GHOST STORIES OF THE
LONG BEACH
PENINSULA

GHOST STORIES OF THE LONG BEACH PENINSULA

SYDNEY STEVENS

Haunted
America

Published by Haunted America
A Division of The History Press
Charleston, SC 29403
www.historypress.net

Front Cover: North Head Light House near Cape Disappointment, Washington. *Photo by Richard Dawson.*
Back Cover: *Columbia River Lightship No. 50,* grounded on Benson Beach in 1899. *Courtesy of Washington State Parks*; The Shelburne Inn, in Seaview, Washington, since 1896. *Photo by Sydney Stevens.*

First published 2014

Manufactured in the United States

ISBN 978.1.62619.730.5

Library of Congress CIP data applied for.

Notice: The information in this book is true and complete to the best of our knowledge. It is offered without guarantee on the part of the author or The History Press. The author and The History Press disclaim all liability in connection with the use of this book.

This book is dedicated to Mrs. Crouch, the preacher's wife, who moved into the Oysterville Baptist Parsonage in 1892, died under mysterious circumstances in 1893 and has remained in residence in the house across from the Oysterville Church ever since.

CONTENTS

FOREWORD

At the heart of any community are its stories. Museums collect photographs, objects and ephemera in order to tell those stories within our walls. We gather facts, research the objects and display them, all with the hope that they give the viewer a sense of place and communicate what is unique about our community. Photographs and objects are wonderful "things," but it takes a writer to convey the character of the distinctive place in which those things exist—the place that touches our emotions, transports us to another time and makes us truly understand how people lived in the past.

Sydney Stevens holds a unique position on the Long Beach Peninsula. Her deep roots here have given her access to the most closely held stories, and her curious nature enables her to reveal the unusual amidst the practicalities of everyday life. After reading her stories, those dusty oil lamps begin to glimmer, and those stiff studio portraits of our forebears become embedded with new meaning. A trip to the museum or the attic will never be quite the same.

Betsy Millard, Director
Columbia Pacific Heritage Museum, Ilwaco

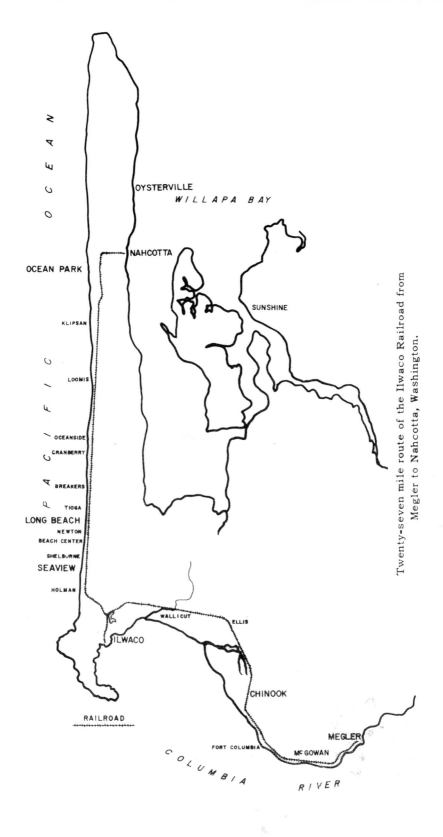

OYSTERVILLE

WILLAPA BAY

OCEAN PARK

NAHCOTTA

SUNSHINE

KLIPSAN

LOOMIS

OCEANSIDE

CRANBERRY

BREAKERS

TIOGA

LONG BEACH

NEWTON

BEACH CENTER

SHELBURNE

SEAVIEW

HOLMAN

WALLICUT

ELLIS

ILWACO

CHINOOK

RAILROAD

MEGLER

FORT COLUMBIA

McGOWAN

COLUMBIA

RIVER

O C E A N

P A C I F I C

Twenty-seven mile route of the Ilwaco Railroad from Megler to Nahcotta, Washington.

PREFACE

On the Long Beach Peninsula—isolated and nearly surrounded as we are by the Columbia River, the Pacific Ocean and Willapa Bay—past and present move as fluidly as the tides that lap our shores. Perhaps that's because so many of us have roots that go back to the beginning of Euro-American settlement—to the boom and bust years of the mid-nineteenth century when law and order was of the Wild West variety, family closets were meant for skeletons and conversation was the major entertainment during the long, stormy winters.

So it is that I live in a household that speaks of the resident ghost as though she were a member of the family. We don't talk about her much, though, and I can't say that all of us actually "believe," but she certainly is a convenient explanation for any of the mysterious events that happen in our more-than-a-century-old house.

Not long ago, and much to my astonishment, I found that other residents of the Peninsula also live with ghosts! The stories were as varied as the people who told them, and each provided a unique view of the past. As an author and historian specializing in local history, I was intrigued.

The North Beach (now called Long Beach) Peninsula Railroad map from Thomas E. Jessett's *Clamshell Railroad*, printed in 1967. *Courtesy of Peninsula Office and Art Supplies.*

After many interviews and much research, I wrote up a number of those tales. They were published in 2008 as a series in our local weekly newspaper, the *Chinook Observer*. Two years later, I put them in "virtual form" as an e-book, believing that the amorphous quality of cyberspace might lend itself to my ghostly subject.

For this book, I have added newly discovered information to several of the stories and included two new stories, which have come to my attention only recently. As with all the very best stories with history at their core, these may leave readers with the urge to learn more. Or so I hope.

ACKNOWLEDGEMENTS

In small communities like those on the Long Beach Peninsula, collaboration is what we do best. It is a skill that takes many forms—a quick conversation at the grocery store, the distribution of information at a meeting or a bit of friendly gossip over the back fence. We pool our knowledge and perpetuate our memories in a never-ending exchange of ideas.

This book is a collaborative effort. Some of the tales have been told and retold—around the parlor fireplace or at a grade school sleepover. Some have only been whispered from generation to generation until, finally, the time came to speak aloud about things not fully understood. I wish to thank all of those who shared their stories with me and who agreed that I could share them with my readers.

For telling me their ghost stories, I would like to thank Sarah "Sally" Sherwood Abernathy, Ann Sherwood Anderson, Jenelle Berry, David Campiche, Marilyn Casey, Ron Cox, Mike Dutchuk, Candy Glenn, Erin Glenn, Frank Glenn III, Frank "Sonny" Glenn IV, Pete Heckes, Ruby Heckes, Jennifer Lonergan, Nanci Main, Greta McDougall, Sharon Miller, Angela Pierce, Gordon Schoewe and Bev Smith.

For research and additional information, I am grateful to Ron Biggs, Barbara Christian, Tom Downer, Ellen Loomis McMurry, Betsy Millard, Barbara Minard, JoAnne Risely, Ken Ross, Kathleen Sayce, Stan Sonntag, Sandra Tellvik, Dorothy Trondsen Williams, Stephen Wood and, most especially, my cousin Ralph Jeffords.

For photographs, I extend special thanks to Sarah Abernathy, Ann Sherwood Anderson, Jon Christian, Richard Dawson, Tom Downer, Candy Glenn, Nanci Main, Nyel Stevens, Dorothy Trondsen Williams and the Columbia Pacific Heritage Museum, the Espy Family Archives, the Oregon Historical Society, the Pacific County Historical Society, Peninsula Office and Art Supplies and Washington State Parks.

Special thanks also to Larry Murante for allowing me to reprint the lyrics to "The Ballad of Mrs. Crouch."

INTRODUCTION

E veryone loves a ghost story. Whether told during a long, dark, winter power outage or while hunkered around a campfire at the beach, ghost stories are sure to hold the attention of all—believers and skeptics, young and old, dreamers and realists. The more familiar the people and places involved, the more intriguing the stories seem.

The tiny finger of land known as the Long Beach Peninsula in Washington's southwest corner provides the perfect setting for such stories. It is isolated and hard to reach—a three-hour automobile journey from the nearest large city. The thickly wooded forests and marshy bogs provide ideal spots for shadowy mysteries. Population is sparse—almost everyone knows everyone else firsthand, secondhand or by reputation. It's hard to keep secrets or to hide skeletons in closets.

The ghost stories that follow were told to me by my neighbors and friends and, at least one, by a complete stranger. Several had not been shared "outside the family" until now, a carry-over from the days when stories of ghosts were too frightful to tell in anything above a whisper.

These ghosts, though, are all benign. At least one seems to be watching over the members of the household and keeping them safe, even from themselves. Mostly the stories are full of mysteries of unsolved circumstances and unanswered questions. They are the very best kind of ghost stories, for they continue to unfold and grow as the years pass and more information is uncovered. Perhaps readers of *Ghost Stories of the Long Beach Peninsula* will come forward with the answers that will put these unsettled spirits to rest at last.

Throughout these stories, there also runs a bit of ghostly subtext, which is yet another example of how we on the Long Beach Peninsula live in continuing harmony with the past. Our place names, especially the names of this Peninsula and of the bay that defines it, morph back and forth according to generation and to the speaker's roots. Readers will find that some names (the old and the new) are used interchangeably throughout these ghost stories.

Shoalwater Bay was the historic name of the large body of water to the east of the Long Beach Peninsula. It was sighted in 1788 by English trader Captain John Meares, who named it for its extreme shallowness. Little more than a century later, in the 1890s, a group of real estate promoters in the mainland town of South Bend dreamed that ships would someday enter the bay and sail up the Willapa River to their town, causing it to become the "Baltimore of the Pacific." Fearing that ship captains would avoid a bay with a name that meant shallow water, they had the name officially changed from Shoalwater to Willapa. They were unable to change the character of the bay itself, however, and South Bend's dream of maritime greatness did not materialize.

The present-day name of the Peninsula, too, was the result of local promoters. When settlers first began to arrive in Oregon Territory, the only method of getting from inland valleys to the Pacific Ocean was by way of the Columbia River. Travelers named the narrow finger of land jutting north from the river's mouth "North Beach" to differentiate it from beaches to the south. The name was changed to Long Beach Peninsula by early twentieth-century tourism promoters from the Peninsula city of Long Beach. However, the official name remains the North Beach Peninsula, and some residents hope that it can come into popular usage once more.

Like the ghosts of the stories that follow, our knowledge of places and people from years past becomes increasingly dim as time moves forward. It is my hope that *Ghost Stories of the Long Beach Peninsula* will bring some of those memories into sharper focus…at least for a time.

1

MRS. CROUCH,
THE PREACHER'S WIFE

Tap-tap-tap. Tap-a-tap-tap-tap. Tap-tap-tap-tap. Tap.
The bedside clock read 2:15. I'd been "home" scarcely two hours, asleep for maybe an hour and a half, when the noise awakened me. It was a commonplace sound, not scary, but I couldn't think what it might be or even where it was coming from. I was alone in the big Oysterville house.

Tap-tap. Tap-tap.

It was vaguely annoying, but what was really keeping me awake was the fact that I could not identify it. And it was nearby. But where?

I turned on the light. The noise stopped. The familiar room with its pink-flowered wallpaper and old-fashioned furniture looked as I remembered it from childhood when this was my grandparents' home. The visit was my first since my folks had retired here a few months previously. I was to housesit for a few weeks while they were away—a welcome break from the hustle-bustle of city life in California. Here, in "my" room overlooking the dear old Oysterville Church, my thirty or so years of adulthood seemed to evaporate. I was ten years old again, and it was the middle of the night. I turned off the light and drifted toward sleep.

Tap-a-tap. Tap. Tap. Tap.

What *was* that sound? Dad had said there was a squirrel that liked to gallop in the gutters. But wouldn't that be a scritchy-scratchy noise? Besides, I had never heard a squirrel in a rain gutter, and this tapping noise was definitely one I had heard before.

Again, I turned on the light. Again, the noise stopped. Finally, I lay there in the dark actually waiting for the *tap tap tap*. When it came, I tried to pinpoint its source. It seemed to be coming from the next-door bedroom, the one we always thought of as belonging to whoever was youngest in the household at the time. I turned on the light and went to investigate.

A typewriter! Of course! But it was the strangest-looking typewriter I had ever encountered and certainly one I had never seen before. Satisfied that I had pinpointed the cause of the mysterious tapping, I went back to bed and slept soundly the rest of the night.

At this point in the story, people often ask, "Did you put a piece of paper in the typewriter?"

I wish I had been that clever. However, the idea never occurred to me. My concern was to discover the source of the sound, and once my curiosity was satisfied, that was that. In fact, I really didn't think about the incident again until weeks later when it occurred to me to ask my mother where that strange old typewriter came from.

This Printype Oliver Typewriter was patented in 1912, long after Mrs. Crouch lived in Oysterville. *Photo by Sydney Stevens.*

"It was on loan to the Pacific County Historical Society for their museum," she said. "Ruth Dixon, the director, called when she heard I was 'back home' and asked me to come get it."

When I related my experience, she laughed and said, "Oh, that was probably Mrs. Crouch!"

"Who?" I asked. It was then that my mother "introduced" me to the ghost with whom I was to become very familiar over the next forty-plus years.

I should say right here that *I* don't believe in ghosts. Not really. Never mind that I've now known about the ghost in our house for years. And never mind that people I respect and love have had "experiences" with our ghost. Most of all, never mind that I have had several encounters with her myself. I'm not a believer. Really.

THE PREACHER ARRIVES

According to my mother, our ghost had come to Oysterville long ago with her husband, Pastor Josiah Crouch, the new Baptist minister. With them were their infant daughter and Josiah's mother and young brother. They arrived in 1892, almost two generations after the town's founding. By then, Oysterville had already lost its standing as the Pacific County seat and the little, native oysters upon which the town's economy had depended had failed. Most of the population had moved away, and life had settled into a peaceful, rural rhythm marked by the changing of tides and seasons.

A year or so before Pastor and Mrs. Crouch arrived, Major R.H. Espy, the patriarch and a founding father of the little village, had donated some property and $1,500 to build the Baptist church. Up to that time, the Baptists had been congregating at Major Espy's house, which was by far the most commodious in Oysterville. They held their services and prayer meetings there, and between the visits of the minister, members of the congregation took turns preaching, availing themselves of "canned" sermons from the old, leather-bound books in the major's library.

The circuit-riding preachers (or in Oysterville's case, the circuit-*sailing* preachers, for they traveled among nearby communities by boat) also boarded with the Espys on their infrequent visits to Shoalwater Bay. When Pastor Huff took up permanent residence, staying even after his retirement from the ministry, the major decided that a parsonage was in order.

The house just across from Oysterville's Baptist church served as the parsonage from 1892 to 1902. Josiah Crouch was the first pastor to live there. *Courtesy of the Espy Family Archives.*

The Baptist congregation in 1903 in front of the Oysterville Church after Josiah Crouch's tenure as pastor. *Courtesy of the Espy Family Archives.*

He bought the Tom Crellin house, which was conveniently located across the road from the new church. Like many other houses in town, it was vacant; buyers and renters were few and far between. Tom Crellin had moved his family to San Francisco so that he could go into banking. Around town, it was said the Crellins were the only people who came to Oysterville with money and left with even more money. But, even so, Mr. Crellin was glad to have a buyer.

The house consisted of four main rooms downstairs, four upstairs and two add-ons—a washroom and a woodshed. It was built in 1869 from plans brought over by the Crellin brothers from their native Isle of Man and was constructed of redwood lumber on a foundation of fieldstone—materials that had been carried as ballast by the early oyster schooners.

Josiah Crouch was the first minister to occupy the house in its new role as parsonage. Tommy Nelson, a teenager at the time, years later told my uncle, Willard Espy, of the preacher's stay in Oysterville, and Willard recorded his story.

LADIES' MAN

"He was a tall, handsome fellow—had an alpaca overcoat. He could sway the women! Why, he baptized one woman who'd been a Catholic all her life.

"I heard Crouch's wife singing when she was alone, and she could sing like a mockingbird. But when a stranger was around, she had nothing to say. My sister went there once. She said she was kind of embarrassed the way Crouch would talk to her and turn his back on his wife.

"One day, he took his wife and baby on a church call up the Willapa, and their sailboat tipped over. Well, Crouch swam ashore with the baby, but his wife drowned. Well, he was interested in another woman at the time. Well, the sheriff found marks on Mrs. Crouch's neck. Crouch was exonerated, but it got too hot for him, and he left town."

Seemingly, the evidence against the preacher was inconclusive, as he was not arrested. However, his congregation made it known that they were not pleased, and he soon left town—without his mother, his brother or his little girl but (so the rumor persists) with someone else's wife. Some time later he was reported as practicing law in San Francisco!

As for Mrs. Crouch, she is buried in the Fern Hill Cemetery near the place where she drowned.

Over the years, bits and pieces of information about the erstwhile preacher have come to light in old letters and church records found tucked away in the attic of the parsonage. Like clues in a detective story, they paint a tantalizing picture, but in this particular mystery, there are still more questions than answers.

From the *South Bend Journal*, July 28, 1893:

FATAL ACCIDENT
Mrs. Josiah Crouch, of Oysterville
Drowned in the Willapa.
Her Husband and Child Narrowly Escape Meeting the Same Fate
  Mrs. Crouch, wife of Josiah Crouch, pastor of the Baptist church at Oysterville, was drowned in the Willapa River, about a mile below Willapa City, last Saturday morning. Mr. and Mrs. Crouch who had been passing a few days in Willapa, started in a large row boat, at nearly 9 o'clock a.m., to go down the river and make a call on Stephen Brown's family. They took with them their little daughter, aged 17 months. Mr. Crouch did the rowing. When they arrived near the Brown place they concluded to put in at George Whitcomb's landing, which they had just passed, and Mrs. Crouch asked her husband to let her row. She handed the baby to him and they started to exchange seats. In this proceeding she tripped, or somehow lost her balance; the boat lurched violently and she was thrown into the water. The rebound threw Mr. Crouch and the child overboard. He could not swim a stroke but he clung to the little one and managed to grasp the side of the boat and so support himself while he kept the child's head above water. Mrs. Crouch, also unable to swim had disappeared. The husband waited a few moments for a sign of her, and then with his feet and legs began to propel the boat to shore. He had nearly reached the bank when he saw, or thought he saw, at some distance below, his wife's head appear a second above the surface. Getting upon the land he ran to the Whitcomb house and alarmed the occupants. The neighbors were hastily summoned and soon many men were out on the river in boats dragging with garden rakes and other implements for the unfortunate woman. The tide was very low, still running out but almost at the turn. The hat worn by Mrs. Crouch came to the surface and was first seen by Henry Stevens. At 11 o'clock, two hours after the accident, the body was brought up, near the middle of the river, a short distance below the spot where the boat was overturned. It was conveyed to Willapa and on Sunday buried in Fern Hill cemetery, Rev. E.L. Hughes conducting the obsequies. The attendance at the funeral service and to the grave was very large.

Mrs. Crouch was about 21 years of age, a bright and amiable woman and was much beloved by her acquaintances. The family had resided in Oysterville about nine months, having removed thither from Arkansas.

The blow is a terrible one to Mr. Crouch, whose misfortune and whose agonized state of mind elicits much sympathy throughout the county.

Since the drowning…a good deal of talk injuriously affecting her husband has been going on throughout the county. The scandal grew to such proportions that Prosecuting Attorney Egbert concluded that the only way to allay it was by an examination of the remains of the deceased… The body of the deceased was exhumed and in the presence of all, the skull was subjected to an examination by the physicians. The result of the inspection is here given:

We, the undersigned physicians hereby certify that at your request we attended in person at the grave of Mrs. Josiah Crouch (relict of Rev. Crouch) who was taken from the water near Willapa where she was alleged to have drowned; that the body of said woman was exhumed in our presence; that we made an examination of the skull on said body and the tissues surrounding the skull and found all the cranial bones intact, and no evidence therein of any fracture; or blows; that the surrounding tissue was in such an advanced state of decomposition that it was impossible to determine whether any blows had been inflicted upon the skull; that on account of the advanced state of decomposition of the tissues of the whole body, we concluded a further examination futile as nothing in reference to any violence, if any were used upon said body, could be determined by such examination.

J.C. Gosnell M.D.
W. Gruwell M.D.

By the following week, however, the *South Bend Journal*'s tone had changed considerably. The headlines on August 4, 1893, read:

INVESTIGATION
A Coroner's Inquest Into the Drowning of Mrs. Crouch
The Testimony and the Verdict.
Alleged Need of Further Inquiry.

A long article follows, giving the total testimony taken on July 29 at a second inquest and concluding with the jury's verdict:

We, the jury, after having been duly impaneled and sworn and having heard all the evidence produced thereat, find: That the deceased Sarah Angeline Crouch came to her death on the 15th day of July 1893 by drowning in the Willapa river, near the town of Willapa, into which river she was precipitated from a row boat, by some means described by her husband, the only living witness of it, and purely accidental.

No documentation remains concerning exactly when Pastor Crouch left town or with whom. However, to this day, rumors continue to circulate that he left suddenly without his daughter and with another man's wife. Undoubtedly, the following letter that arrived at the Oysterville post office in late November fanned the flames of speculation to fever pitch.

November 22, 1893
Topeka, Kansas
D.O. Parmeter
Post Master
Oysterville Wash.
Sir:
...I am the ferst [sic] wife of one Josiah Crouch. I was married to him the 5 day of August in 1885 at St. Joseph, Mo. County Buccanan [sic]. In 1888 he left me at Havensville Kans and I understand that he went to Ark. In 1889 he married a woman by the name of Tedden at Gladstone Ark as I had too [sic] letters from D.P. Tedden the father of his last wife. I have a little girl 7 years old. I have written some letter [sic] to Ilwaco with my one [own] handis [hands] no forgery. I have send [sic] letter [sic] a copy of Mr. Teddens letter and a stat ment [statement] nad [and] copy of the married [sic] lissen [license] to T.H. Parks at Ilwaco Wash if you wish to see thum [sic] you can write to him.
yours respectfully Mrs. Tillie Crouch

Just a few days later, in a letter posted from Oysterville on November 27, 1893, Julia Jefferson Espy wrote to her three oldest children who were attending high school in Centralia. She told them about the arrival of the replacement preacher and of the latest tidings concerning Mr. Crouch:

At Sealand Mr. Huff had met Mr. Ireland, wife & child 3 years old who had come to hold meetings with the pastorate in view. He too is a Missouri man and shows it as plainly as Crouch did but does not seem at all like

Julia Jefferson Espy, clerk of the Baptist church, kept careful records concerning Josiah Crouch and his unfortunate experiences in Pacific County. *Courtesy of the Espy Family Archives.*

Mr. Crouch. I do not think he appears as smart a man as Mr. Crouch but is one who will talk better though rather odd…

I do not think we will be able to keep him as the Willapa church will not be able to do anything and this church alone is less able than last year. Mr. Crouch is in Eastern Oregon & is thinking of becoming a General Missionary.

WOLF IN SHEEP'S CLOTHING

The following week, on December 3, 1893, Julia again wrote her children, this time with some chagrin:

You asked about Crouch. We think we have reason to fear we have harbored a wolf in sheep's clothing. His mother rec'd a letter from him yesterday

25

saying he "had learned that a warrant was out for his arrest and while he was not afraid to stand trial, he believed that they wanted to get hold of him to mob him, so he was going to parts unknown."

He could not have taken a surer way to convince people of his guilt.

His mother will go back to her sister as quick as she can get the money to go on. Crouch sent her $5 & told her to sell his things to raise more. As he had nothing when he came and is owing your father more than the furniture cost, she cannot raise anything that way. I feel very sorry for her but do not know anything I can say to comfort. What sorrow a child can bring to a parent, but we are glad that though he may be a scoundrel, it will not destroy the power of the truth. So far as his preaching was in accord with the Bible, it will be blessed.

More evidence that Crouch may, indeed, have been a "wolf in sheep's clothing" came in an envelope addressed "To the clerk of the first Babtist [*sic*] Church at Oysterville Washington." The letter, though written without benefit of punctuation, clearly conveys the writer's distress concerning his own experience with Pastor Crouch:

December 6, '93

Dear Brother in Christ

I write to you to find out if brother Crouch is with you yet he left hear [sic] a little over a year ago and we heard from him a few times he borrowed ten dollars of me to help take him their [sic] he promised he would send it just as soon as he got their [sic] I have written to him for it but he has never sent me but 2 dolars [sic] of it yet and I am a poor man I borrowed the money to let him have it and he new [sic] I borrowed it I dont think he is cheating me just think he forgot perhaps you will no [sic] if he can not possible pay it or if he don't try it seems he ough [sic] to be able to pay it in one year I am sory for we though [sic] well of Brother Crouch he staid at our home several days or weeks we though [sic] his word as good as any thing but it has not proved so if its not asking too much of you pleas [sic] answer me this letter show it to him if he is with you and you want to he owes me 8 dolars [sic] yet yors [sic] Brother in Christ, M.A. Childres Wamego, Kansas

HEARTBROKEN MOTHER

In Julia's next weekly letter to her children in Centralia, on December 10, 1893, she wrote:

> *Your father let Mrs. Crouch have the money to pay her way & she started back to Lincoln, Nebraska, Friday. I never saw a more heartbroken woman. I wish my boys could have seen her; it ought to be a lesson and shows what sorrow a child can cause a parent. She was so much prostrated I fear she will be bedfast before she reaches friends. She said she thought he would be able to prove his innocence but we keep hearing something new.*

A letter from the Office of the County Clerk of Buchanan County, Missouri, was dated December 13, 1893, and addressed to Mrs. R.H. Espy, clerk of the Baptist church, Oysterville, Washington. Apparently, it was in answer to an inquiry made on behalf of the Baptist congregation to corroborate the claim of Crouch's first wife, Tillie.

> *Madam,*
> *On examination of the books in the Recorder's office of this county I find that Josiah Crouch was married to Tillie Lindgren August 6th 1885*

In 1893, the only north–south road on the Long Beach Peninsula was the IR&N. *Courtesy of the Espy Family Archives.*

by Rev. C.I. Vanderenter of this city. If you want a certified copy of the marriage certificate it will cost $1.50 fee to Recorder.

Very Truly, Wallis Young

Shortly before Christmas, on December 20, 1893, a letter was written to Postmaster Parmeter. It is unsigned but appears to be from a friend, possibly an Oysterville resident who had moved to California.

Los Angeles, December 20, 1893

Friend Bub:

I recd your welcome letter yesterday morning. I first saw your man here about 10 or 12 days ago or thought it was him at one of the Employment office [sic] here. He looked so seedy and rough that I did not know whether it was he or not, but spoke to one of the fellows here about him. And he said that he heard the man say that he was just off the train from Kansas only 2 hours. I saw him yesterday going around with a small valise. Seemed to be peddling. He was better dressed and looked exactly like Crouch. I met him this morning face to face on the sidewalk and he gave me quite a stare. Saw him this afternoon again and would have met and passed him. But I crossed the street so as not to meet him. I never liked the looks of the man. Thought he was a skunk. I have seen nothing of the girl. He was always alone. Wears a black soft hat with brim shoved up on either side. It is rather old.

IMPOSTER

The Baptist congregation deliberated long and hard about their responsibility in regard to the preacher. Entries in the clerk's record book stated:

December 21st 1893

Oysterville Bapt. Church met…after the regular prayer meeting.

Remarks by Bro. Espy & others concerning Josiah Crouch and his conduct as to the fact that it was not in keeping with his position as Reverend of a Baptist Church and a Minister of the Gospel. Motion and seconded that the Clerk send notices to the various Baptist Papers of the coast publishing Crouch to the world as an imposter. Motion carried. Motion that the motion be reconsidered and laid over until the regular Covenant Meeting. Motion carried.

J.T. Huff Moderator; D.O. Parmeter, Clerk

At a follow-up meeting:

> *Jan. 13, 1894*
>
> *Oysterville Baptist Church met in regular Covenant meeting at 7 p.m…*
>
> *Charges of the crimes against the Church, his fellow beings, the laws of the land and against God Almighty of Bigamy, obtaining money under false pretenses, and of having left his mother, brother and daughter without means of support and requesting them to go east without it were preferred against Josiah Crouch by R.H. Espy. Motion by Bro. Ireland that Crouch be notified to appear at the next regular meeting and answer to the charges either to defend himself or plead guilty, and that if he did not he would be expelled. Motion carried.*

The last bit of information found, at least thus far, concerning Josiah Crouch is in a letter dated 1897, postmarked San Francisco. It was written to Julia and Major Espy by their eldest son, Ed Espy, an attorney in Northern California:

> *You ask about Crouch. He was in for 15 or 20 minutes and talked about people in Washington etc. He is now living in Stockton* [California]. *His mother and child are living in Los Angeles. He has married again and, I think he said that he had a child.*

Unfortunately, little has come to light about Sarah Crouch herself, though many people have had "experiences" with her. For a number of years after my grandparents died in the 1950s, the house was not regularly occupied. It was during those years that people often reported hearing a woman's sweet voice singing hymns in the house that was once the parsonage.

Shortly after my typewriter experience, Noel and Pat Thomas and Dennis and Kathie Crabb were in the house visiting my folks. Just as my mother was telling them the story of Mrs. Crouch, the lid to an old incense burner jumped across the room onto the floor with a loud clunk.

"It was lead or some other heavy metal and was sitting up on top of a bookcase," remembers Pat. "There was no reasonable explanation for it taking off like that. It was eerie."

In addition to these "actual" events, poor Sarah Crouch gets the blame for a lot of other unexplained happenings—like whenever one of a pair of socks is missing, someone is sure to say, "Mrs. Crouch must have done it."

If only I had thought to put a piece of paper in that old typewriter! Perhaps I could now be telling the "rest of the story" about Mrs. Crouch, the preacher's wife.

The lid of this metal incense burner measures three inches in diameter and two inches in height and weighs almost three ounces. *Photo by Sydney Stevens.*

...AND THE BEAT GOES ON...

As is the custom at our house when we have overnight visitors, we were enjoying my husband Nyel's made-from-scratch sourdough waffles and listening to Gregorian chants the morning after our friend Larry Murante's first stay in Oysterville. During the leisurely breakfast, I jokingly asked Larry if he had experienced any unusual visitors during the night, a question that naturally led to the story of Mrs. Crouch.

Larry grew more and more silent as the tale continued, and not silent in a good way. It seemed to us that he rushed through the rest of his meal, packed up hurriedly and left a bit too soon. During the goodbyes, as we urged him to come back again, he said he certainly would, but he thought he would stay at a motel. Or bring his wife. He didn't want to risk an encounter with a ghost.

But Larry is a singer-songwriter in Seattle, and the story of the preacher's wife stayed in his thoughts. By the time of his next visit, this time with his lovely wife, Karen, he had written a song about Mrs. Crouch. Perhaps his twist at the end was his own way of coming to terms with the ghost in the parsonage.

The Ballad of Mrs. Crouch
Larry Murante

There was a ghost
In my bedroom
She died in 1892

Her husband the preacher
Could only save the child
He said he did all he could do

She washed ashore
With bumps and bruises
And marks around her neck

And the sheriff had to rule it an accident
But he always wondered in retrospect

CHORUS:
But I was never scared
Of Mrs. Crouch
When I was a boy
She was the ghost
That roamed our house

I was never scared
Of Mrs. Crouch
At night I'd wake
And I'd hear her singing there
When I'd open my eyes
She'd vanish in thin air

Most of the oysters
Were gone from Oysterville
By the time the Crouches came to stay
At this parsonage
And the brand-new church
For the ones here left to pray

This new preacher's wife
Pure innocence
With a voice calming as rain

In my room
She'd sing her little girl to sleep
When the daylight began to wane

(Chorus)

They found out
That the preacher was really no preacher
He was not a righteous man
He had two other wives in wait...

Far away in another land...
He was not a righteous man

Here I stand, years later
Outside this parsonage of my youth
I moved away from here
Thirty years ago
But I still think about you

Your child, my mother's mother
And I'm your great-grandson
I came back here to tell you
That it's alright to leave this place
'Cause your work down here is done

(Chorus)

2

MYSTERIOUS TRAGEDY AT SPRAGUE'S HOLE

Sprague's Hole was one of those wonderful swampy places that kids love to fool around in—the kind of places that were common on the Peninsula before dikes and drainage ditches dried things out. It was where boys hunted pollywogs, kept an eye on a beaver dam or—in the case of Phillip Brooks, Victor Slingerland and Lester Young—went to gather up the snipe that Lester's older brother had shot earlier that day. Sprague's Hole was located somewhere between Ocean Park and Nahcotta. Nowadays, no one can remember just where.

"I don't really recall ever hearing about Sprague's Hole," says Dorothy Trondsen Williams. "It was probably one of those places my friend Bobby Venable and I were not to go to. But we probably went anyway."

Dorothy was born in 1926, fourteen long years after the 1912 tragedy at Sprague's Hole—a lifetime ago to a child—and neither Dorothy nor her brother, John Trondsen, remembers ever hearing so much as a whisper about it. But Dorothy does remember the Brooks House in Ocean Park, and it was one of the Brooks boys who was involved in the mysterious accident at Sprague's Hole.

"I was in that house many, many times," says Dorothy. "It's the house where the Venables lived, and in the early 1930s, Bobby Venable was my best friend. I think they rented the house. We always called it the 'Brooks House,' but I didn't know much about that family. They were before my time."

The house, now owned by Nanci Main, was built in the late 1800s or early 1900s for John and Anna Brooks. Both 1895 and 1915 have been cited as dates for the construction, though neither date fits exactly with the other meager facts about the Brooks family.

Anna and John were married in 1901. Would they have built their house six years prior? After 1912, though, there were only three in the Brooks family. Would they have built their sizeable, ten-room house three years later?

MASTER CARPENTERS

Whatever the date, it was built by one or more of the Matthews men; again, no one is quite sure of the facts. Stephen Adelbert Matthews had built and lived in the big house on Bay Avenue—the house that in recent years has been known as the "Whalebone House." He was a well-respected carpenter in the late 1800s and early 1900s and is said to have built more than half of the summer cottages that went up in Ocean Park during those years. If the Brooks House was built in 1895, it was probably S.A. Matthews who did the building.

Nanci has heard, however, that the house was built by the "Matthews brothers." By 1915, S.A. Matthews was sixty-three years old and his children—five sons and a daughter—were grown. Of his sons, both Zhetley "Zip" and Thedford "Ted" were carpenters, and both may also

The Brooks House, built at the turn of the twentieth century, has been a part of Ocean Park's charming streetscape for as long as anyone can remember. *Courtesy of Nanci Main.*

Stephen Adelbert Matthews posed as the "Old Mariner" for photographer Charles Fitzpatrick, a picture now used as the logo for the Pacific County Historical Society. *Courtesy of the Columbia Pacific Heritage Museum.*

have had a hand in building some of the beach cottages, perhaps even the Brooks House.

Regardless of the builder(s), the house has unusual characteristics. "I've moved a lot in my life," says Nanci, "and the rule of thumb seems to be that it takes about a year to feel really comfortable in a house that is new to you.

Not so in the Brooks House! I knew before I even went through the door that I would find it a safe and reassuring space. I felt embraced by the house immediately."

Perhaps that is the way young Phillip Brooks felt about the house, too. And perhaps that is why Nanci has the feeling that he has lingered there for the many years since the tragedy that befell him.

THE TRAGEDY

Ilwaco Tribune, *Ilwaco, Washington, Saturday, April 6, 1912*

SAD DROWNING AT OCEAN PARK
Three Bright School Boys Meet Death in Sprague's Hole

Ocean Park received the most distressful visitation within the memory of its oldest citizen on Thursday evening when three of its bright and promising little school boys, Victor Slingerland, aged 12, Phillip Brooks, aged 10, and Lester Young, aged 12, met death by being drowned.

The little boys were going home from school and stopped at the Sprague's hole to play in a boat and no one knows just how the accident occurred. It is supposed that when the three boys were paddling around in the slough where the water is deepest, the boat was capsized. Phillip Brooks and Victor Slingerland probably drowned at once, while Lester in some manner reached shore, but in such an exhausted condition as to be unable to help himself, and died from the effects of the exposure soon after being found lying on the bank in an unconscious condition, in which condition he remained until death came.

The bodies of Victor and Phillip were recovered from the bottom of the slough by Mr. Slingerland soon after that of Lester had been found on the bank.

The father of Lester was a former teacher of the school at Ocean Park, but is now traveling for an Eastern shoe house, and was at the Perkins Hotel in Portland Friday morning when told of the accident over the phone by Mr. Howerton.

The parents of the children all reside at Ocean Park and the dreadful accident has cast the black shadow of sorrow over the entire Peninsula.

The Methodist Chapel was Ocean Park's first place of worship. *Courtesy of the Espy Family Archives.*

The funeral was held on Sunday morning in the Methodist Chapel in Ocean Park. A follow-up newspaper article said:

> *Mr. Brooks was privileged to be at home in the sad bereavement, he having been located stopping at the Hotel Perkins in Portland, and informed about 2 a.m. Friday of the irreparable loss. He arrived home on Saturday morning's train. Mr. Brooks and wife and family are naturally very much broken up over the sad event and have the sympathy of the entire community.*

Now, nearly one hundred years later, memories of the Brooks family are few and far between. Mrs. Brooks was a teacher at Nahcotta School, Mr. Brooks was a traveling salesman and there was one other son, Russell—these are "facts" that seem to be true.

AUNTY BROOKS

Ellen Loomis McMurry was born in 1921 and lived on Bay Avenue, just a block or two from the Brooks House. Her mother knew Mrs. Brooks well, and for that reason, Ellen called her "Aunty" Brooks—a term of respect for female friends of the family.

"I loved Aunty Brooks. She had the most beautiful flower garden," says Ellen, "and she used to give me bouquets. I remember once that she had given me a bunch of flowers, and as I turned and headed home, she said, 'Ellen…' in that special tone of voice that adults use to gently reprimand children. I remember that I turned and looked at her, knowing exactly what she wanted, but for some reason, I had a stubborn streak and refused to say anything.

"Finally she said, 'Ellen, you must say thank you.' She waited, but I remained silent. So she took back the bouquet, and I ran home in tears. I just don't know what got into me!" she laughs.

"I also remember that Aunty Brooks would come over to the house to give me a bath if my mother was ill. I can still see that little tin tub that we had in the kitchen! I think Aunty Brooks must have been a very kind and helpful neighbor."

Ellen does not remember ever hearing about Phillip Brooks or of his tragic death at Sprague's Hole. "I only remember one son," she says. "He was a big boy. Of course, I was a very little girl then. I suppose he must have been twelve or thirteen. I don't remember anything at all about Mr. Brooks."

Anna Brooks died on August 7, 1925. According to her death certificate, she was married to John Brooks, but no son named Russell is mentioned. On the other hand, her obituary lists Russell as her sole survivor—no mention of husband John. There seem to be no clear answers to most of the questions about the Brooks family.

Nanci, however, is very clear about the Brooks House itself. "There is definitely an energy in this house," she says. "It has a feeling of stability. During the worst storms, it seems absolutely solid—no creaking or shaking. And I feel it evokes the connectedness of the community."

Indeed, several longtime community members, past and present, lived in the Brooks House between the time of Anna's death in 1925 and when Nanci bought the house sixty years later. For some years, it was a rental. Dorothy Williams's friends the Venables rented it for a while; later, Carl and Bessie Asanuma and their daughters Carlyn and Susan lived there.

As far as it is known, the house remained in the Brooks family as a rental until 1956, when Carole and Jack Wiegardt purchased it for back taxes at an auction on the steps of the courthouse.

"We lived there until 1963 when the Ocean Park Fire Hall was built kitty-corner across the street," says Carole. "The siren was positioned evenly with our second story, and in those days, anyone could go push the fire alarm button, which was located on the outside wall of the fire hall. That, plus the fact that our family was growing, prompted us to move into Nahcotta to the house by the post office. Jack's mother, Lillie, bought the Brooks House from us."

THE DOMINO EFFECT

"The Wiegardts' move created a bit of a domino effect among the households of Ocean Park and Nahcotta," remembers Kathleen Sayce. "Our family lived in the house to the north, just behind the Wiegardts'. The adults had constructed a child-sized gate in the fence, which separated our yards. My sister Cyndi, my brother Jim and I and the oldest two Wiegardt kids—Jon and Liz—used that gate a lot.

"It had a high threshold, maybe sixteen inches, so that the littlest Wiegardt kids couldn't get through easily. And I remember how we older ones giggled when the adults occasionally used the gate. They had to bend way over and step way up. Our laughter wasn't at them but at the pure delight of knowing that it was *our* own special gate!

"When Lillie decided that she would move 'into town' to Jack and Carole's place, my folks decided that they would move 'out of town' to Lillie's place! (My dad, Clyde, still lives there.) Then mom's mother and her husband, Ruth and Renee Garin, decided to buy our house 'in town.' Every time one household emptied a box, it went to the next household to be filled, moved and emptied," she laughs.

"After we moved, I doubt that the little gate was ever used again. In fact, I think that Lillie had it boarded up."

For a while after Lillie died in 1970, the Brooks House was rented out again, often to oystermen and their families. The succession becomes a bit foggy until 1974, when the Wiegardts sold the house to Dean Ellsworth who, in turn, sold it to Nanci in 1985.

"I wasn't even intending to buy a house," says Nanci. "I was driving by and saw the sign. The house seemed to call to me. At that time, it was known in the community as the 'Wiegardt House,' and there was a 'W' on the gate. The 'W' has long since fallen off, but I've retained the gate, even though I had to replace the fence itself. To me, the gate is another community connection."

Until Nanci replaced the fence, the other gate—the children's gate in back—was still there, too. "Carole Wiegardt pointed it out to me early on," says Nanci. "I don't remember now whether it was still operable."

"From the time I moved in, people were so generous in sharing their memories about the house and its place in their lives. My nearest neighbors—Ed Chellis and Elsie Maynard, now both gone—were so welcoming. Elsie showed me her marvelous quilt collection and made me a standing offer of the old-fashioned pie cherries from her tree.

"Even the siren at the fire hall has seemed friendly. I once lived in a house that burned to the ground. I lost everything—dishes, photographs, mementos from the past. So when I hear the siren go off at night and then within minutes hear the firemen going off in the fire rigs, I feel a great sense of comfort and gratitude.

"I have no doubt that my house reflects the friendly quality of the neighborhood, just as it expresses the personalities of those who have lived within its walls. It is such a loving, generous-spirited house. I know it has many stories to tell, if only it could," says Nanci.

"But there is one room that is much different from all the others. It's the upstairs back bedroom. There is a stillness there. A sort of quiet waiting. I'm sure it must have been young Phillip's room.

"Another thing—despite the sturdiness of the house, even during big storms, there are often times that doors, especially the trapdoor to the attic, mysteriously open as if someone has entered or left but has neglected to shut the door behind them. Much like a ten-year-old boy might do!

"Not long after I moved in, a friend—a psychic friend—came to visit me. No sooner had she walked in the door than she said to me, 'There are thirteen spirits in this house. You are surrounded by love!'

"I don't know if there are thirteen spirits in the house," Nanci muses. "But certainly there are a group of them. Perhaps one is Mrs. Brooks. Ed Chellis lived right across the street. He told me that he remembered going to the Brooks House when he was a boy to see someone who had been 'laid out' after they had died. That was common in those days—to have the viewing of the body in the living room of the deceased. I imagine it was Mrs. Brooks who he was paying his respects to."

Nanci says she has never actually seen any of the spirits in the house, but she is well aware of their proximity. "Sometimes I'll catch a movement out of

THE BEST TEACHER IN THE COUNTY

From 1915 to 1918, Anna Brooks taught at the Oysterville School. My grandparents, Helen and Harry Espy, thought she was the best teacher that the school ever had. Since their seven children had attended the Oysterville School between 1905 and 1923, and since my grandfather had himself been a pupil at the Oysterville School from 1882 to 1890, their basis for comparison was considerable. In their opinion, Anna Brooks was without peer.

By the time their youngest child, Dale (my mother), was ready for the eighth grade in 1923, Mrs. Brooks was teaching at the Nahcotta School. So, it was decided that Dale would go to the Nahcotta School for the year. I often heard her tell the story:

"Mrs. Brooks had been my two older brothers' teacher at 'the big kids' school' in Oysterville, but by the time I was in the upper grades, she was teaching at the Nahcotta School. The folks felt that Mrs. Brooks was the best teacher in the county, and they must have thought that I would have trouble passing that eighth grade exam if I was taught by anyone else. So, instead of attending school in Oysterville for my final year of grammar school, I rode my horse the four miles from Oysterville to Nahcotta every morning that it wasn't too stormy.

"At school, I'd take off the bridle and hang it in the cloak room (there was no saddle to worry about as my father thought them dangerous for children), give the horse a slap so he'd go home and then, in the afternoon, I'd catch a ride back to Oysterville on Mr. Lehman's mail wagon. On rainy days, I'd have to leave an hour earlier to go with Willard and Ed in the Model T, which they drove to get to high school in Ilwaco. There was no school bus in those days. I'd spend that extra hour with our friend Deane Nelson, who worked at the store in Nahcotta."

Mom passed her eighth grade exam without incident and went on to graduate from high school and from the University of Redlands. Mrs. Brooks always got all of the credit!

When Anna Brooks (back, far right) taught at the Oysterville School from 1915 to 1919, she was part of the Oysterville Sewing Circle. *Courtesy of the Espy Family Archives.*

In this 1924–1925 Nahcotta School picture, Mrs. Brooks stands second from right in the back row. *Courtesy of the Espy Family Archives.*

the corner of my eye, but when I turn to look, there is nothing unusual there. And many, many times I have felt an icy draft of air, yet my house is always warm and airtight—there are no drafty places. It's always a comforting energy—never scary.

"I believe that buildings reflect the lives of the people who have lived and worked in them. The people who lived in the Brooks House over the years were an integral part of our community, and I think that's what I feel in the house. To me, the house stands for the sense of responsibility and commitment that those who lived here felt for the community. And that's the kind of energy that those good people left behind in the house. I'm grateful to those folks; I love my home and I'm so glad it called out to me all those years ago!"

3
NED OSBORN, JILTED LOVER

When I first moved to Oysterville some forty years ago, the old Ned Osborn House was owned by Norm Dutchuk and his wife, Dolores. In a village known for its "characters," Norm was among the most colorful. In fact, when he died some fifteen years later, Dolores had "The Mad Russian of Oysterville" carved on his tombstone—"not mad in the sense of angry or insane," their son Mike is quick to explain. "More the wild-and-crazy-guy kind of mad."

Norm was a fun-loving, people and party person. A salesman in the Portland, Oregon area, he frequently offered a getaway to his Oysterville house as a bonus to his clients. Invariably, they became friends, and during the thirty or forty weekends a year that Norm himself was in residence, there was often a party going on. If the weather was good, the party was more than likely in the front yard, and Norm's end of our quiet village street could be said to be "a little boisterous," perhaps reminiscent of Oysterville's rip-roaring pioneer days of one hundred years past.

A Matching Glass Eye

Not only did Norm have a larger-than-life capacity for fun, he looked the part of a character, too. An inveterate hunter, he had lost an eye from a stray pellet on a pheasant-hunting expedition in eastern Oregon. His

The inscription on the back of Dolores and Norm Dutchuk's imposing tombstone reflects Norm's fun-loving zest for life. *Photo by Sydney Stevens.*

one glass eye, though a good match for his real one, gave him a distinctive, somewhat zany appearance. Mike, with a sense of humor to match his dad's, has kept Norm's glass eyes—there was always a spare—and has plans to place them somewhere in the house, perhaps imbedded in a brick above a doorway, to keep watch over the comings and goings of the household.

It was a Sunday "morning-after" that I met Norm. He came dashing around my Uncle Willard Espy's neighboring cottage where Wede (as Willard was often called), his wife, Louise, and I were having a leisurely cup of mid-morning coffee. "Were we too noisy last night, Wede?"

"Not at all, Norm," Willard chuckled. "In fact, I thought the party broke up a little earlier than usual."

"Yeah, I had to send them all home. That's what I want to talk to you about. Around midnight or so, I went into the house to get another beer, and a man I'd never seen before came down the stairs. It was the damnedest thing. He said to me, 'Get those people the hell out of here.' And I could tell he meant business. So I sent everyone home. I was wondering if you had any idea who that man was."

"What Did He Look Like?"

Willard looked very interested, though somewhat amused, I thought. "Well, what did the man look like?" he asked. "Short or tall? Did he have a beard? How old do you think he was?"

Norm answered each question, elaborating with detail, and at that point I wondered which man, if either, was pulling the other's leg. Or were they both serious? I wish I had listened more closely to Norm's answers, for after some time, Willard said, "You know, I think that was Ned Osborn. At least that's what I remember him looking like when I was a boy."

"Well, that's what I wondered," said Norm. And both men lapsed into silence.

Louise and I, full of curiosity, wanted more information, and at our urging, Norm and Wede told us what they knew of the man who had built and lived in the house that the Dutchuks now owned.

Osborn was born in Kalmar, Sweden, and went to sea as a young boy, along with his good friend, Charles Nelson. The two of them eventually wound up in Oysterville and settled along Fourth Street (now Territory Road) on neighboring parcels of land. Ned went to work as a sailmaker and, in 1873, began building a house for his bride-to-be.

Like many of the old residential buildings of Oysterville, Osborn's house may be classified as carpenter-style architecture. It is a simple, T-shaped plan, of wood-frame construction with a pitched roof and shiplap siding. The covered front porch shelters stacks of stove wood, a barrel full of long-handled garden tools and an old-fashioned porch swing and provides an inviting entryway to the house.

The front door opens directly into the kitchen—a cozy space dominated by a round dining table and a wood cookstove—a room that is obviously the heart of the old structure, for it gives access to all other parts of the house.

More than one hundred years of history and mystery are hidden behind this peaceful-looking old Oysterville house. *Photo by Sydney Stevens.*

To the left are the parlor and the downstairs bedroom; to the right are the pantry and the bathroom. Along the rear wall, next to the kitchen sink and counter, a door opens onto a generous back porch. It is from the kitchen, too, that the stairway leads to the large dormitory-style bedroom above—a room that can sleep as many as twelve, says Mike.

UPSTAIRS NEVER FINISHED

Whether Ned intended to make separate bedrooms upstairs is unclear. As the house was nearing completion, he sent to the "old country" for his true love but learned that she had recently died. Though he lived in the house for the rest of his days, Ned never married, nor did he finish the upstairs portion of the house. Perhaps he had soured on life, Norm and Willard speculated; perhaps that was why he didn't hold much truck with partying into the wee hours.

By the time they had finished telling the tale, both Norm and Willard seemed convinced that the man who had come down from those erstwhile unfinished rooms was Ned Osborn himself, though dead for more than fifty years. Not one of us ever said the word "ghost" or "haunted" or "spirit." The facts as presented by Norm and dignified by Wede's careful questioning seemed to warrant more respect than to be called a "ghost story." However, Ned Osborn became a person of interest in my mind, and when more information about him surfaced many years later, I was intrigued.

It was while I was cleaning out a closet in the Espy family house that I ran across some notes on the back of an old envelope, stamp cancellation date 1947. In my grandfather's familiar, cramped handwriting down the length of the paper, almost in poetic form, was "new" information about Ned and his house!

Ned Osborn House
1872 about
Built by Edward (Ned) Osborn
Batched there all his life
Died of stroke 1906
Alga Fagenstrom (?)
Engaged to & built house
For but engagement was broken.
He never married.

She did years later
Just before the upstairs
Was finished which was
Then never completed.
Wood—rough wood from South Bend
Finished lumber from California

The first thing that struck me was that Ned's sweetheart had apparently jilted him by choice, not through death, and that it wasn't until she married someone else that he gave up hope and stopped working on his house. It also sounded as though the young lady may have been a local girl, not the sweetheart left behind in Sweden of Wede's story. Try as I might, however, I could not find anyone by that name in nineteenth-century Pacific County. The nearest in spelling was "Alma Fagerstrom," who may have been an early student at the Smith Island School, located on the south end of a wooded knoll on the west bank of the lower Naselle River.* No other name came close.

REMEMBERING NED?

But more astonishing to me than the new facts about Ned's intended was the date of Old Ned's death—four years *prior* to Willard's birth date. Oh, that Willard! "Remembered" Ned, indeed!

When I confronted Willard with this discrepancy of dates, his eyes opened wide. "Really?" he said. "I'm absolutely sure I remember him!" And he said it so convincingly that I could actually empathize with the feeling. Many are the stories that I have heard so many times that I truly believe I witnessed the events myself. Still...

Norm and Wede remained friends for all the many years they were neighbors in Oysterville. Willard was fond of telling about Norm's prowess as a Russian dancer and about the time, in front of his own cottage fireplace, Norm had demonstrated his ability to do the high leaps and squatting kicks of the traditional Cossack dance. Willard also remarked from time to time that Norm's late-night partying had all but stopped.

---

* The Naselle River originates in the Willapa Hills and flows generally west, passing the community of Naselle (several miles upriver from the Long Beach Peninsula) before emptying into the southern part of Willapa Bay. The river's name has been variously spelled Nasel and Nasal. According to some scholars, the name comes from the Nisal Indians, a Chinookan tribe formerly residing on the river.

 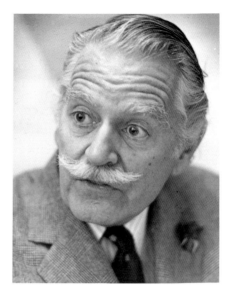

Left: The years have taken their toll on the wooden marker that originally denoted Ned's final resting place at the Oysterville cemetery. *Photo by Sydney Stevens.*

Right: Author and raconteur Willard Espy was a good listener. If he didn't believe the stories Norm told him, he never let on. *Courtesy of the Espy Family Archives.*

Whether or not the two men ever discussed Ned Osborn's visit again, I don't know. Apparently, it wasn't something that Norm often talked about. In fact, when I spoke with Mike recently, it wasn't until I was well into the story that he remembered hearing his dad tell about the man who came down the stairs. As far as Mike knows, there were no further encounters, but for a while, it was not uncommon to hear furniture being moved around upstairs even when all members of the household were present and accounted for—downstairs. Family and friends took for granted that it was Ned.

"All that stopped in the mid-eighties," says Mike. "Ned's wooden grave marker was getting pretty beat up at the cemetery, so my dad replaced it with a replica and brought the original here to the house for safekeeping. We have it in a protected area in the front yard. Ned, of course, is still up at the cemetery, but once his wooden marker came to the house, the upstairs noises stopped."

Mike and I sat and thought about that for a time, much as Norm and Willard had pondered the mysterious visit years before. We didn't come to any grand conclusions—just that maybe Ned Osborn simply wanted someone to care.

4

THE GHOST SHIP *SOLANO*

It's been four or five decades since the *Solano* has made an appearance on the Long Beach Peninsula. Only the oldest generation remembers seeing her, walking right up, climbing on and exploring her. They still talk about her, and even though they know more about Spanish and its pronunciation these days, locals still refer to her as the *Solano* with a long "a." Usually, though, they just refer to her as "the wreck" or "the ghost ship." They know she will be back.

The *Solano* was a 728-ton, four-masted American schooner on her way from San Francisco to Grays Harbor, a bay located forty-five miles north of the mouth of the Columbia River. The first notice of her unscheduled arrival on the Peninsula came early in the morning of February 5, 1907, to the North Beach lifesaving crew at Klipsan Beach, just south of Ocean Park.

The lookout in the station's tower sighted distress signals rising above the low-hanging fog several miles up the beach. The men quickly donned their storm gear and made their way north along the sandy shore, carrying their rescue equipment and lighting the foggy, pre-dawn gloom with their torches.

The surf was exceptionally calm for a winter day, and the surfmen encountered little difficulty in getting the shipwrecked seamen ashore. Even a small dog was rescued from the hapless ship.* On close inspection at low

---

* The dog was adopted by young Willie Taylor of Ocean Park, who named him Solano in honor of the wreck. Two years later, in one of those stranger-than-fiction occurrences, the dog's incessant howling raised the alarm as the French bark *Alice* ran aground, just three miles south of the wrecked *Solano*.

Before running aground near Ocean Park in 1907, the graceful *Solano* held the record for fastest passage from Shanghai to Port Townsend—twenty-four days in 1902. *Courtesy of the Espy Family Archives.*

The crew at the Klipsan Beach Life Saving Station drilled regularly to be ready for shipwreck emergencies along the Peninsula's treacherous coast. *Courtesy of the Espy Family Archives.*

water, the schooner was found to be undamaged, so plans were immediately made to refloat her.

Due to time and tide constraints, it was necessary to wait ten full months for a flood tide of sufficient magnitude to relaunch the vessel. Meanwhile, the captain and crew members continued to live aboard, thus freeing the county wreckmaster from one of his most difficult duties.

As much as possible, it was business as usual for these shipboard guardians. Contemporary reports noted the astonishment of visitors to the beach upon seeing the ship—fully upright and completely landlocked in the sand, often with the crew's clean laundry flapping from the rigging.

Relaunching Attempt

During the interim months, a large salvage crew, under the direction of W.H. Wood of the Hart-Wood Lumber Company, had worked tirelessly to prepare the vessel for relaunching. On the highest tide of December 1907, the task was successfully completed.

The Wreckmaster

This elective office was created by the first Territorial Legislature in 1854 for all counties of Washington Territory that bordered the Pacific Ocean. In 1907, the year the *Solano* wrecked, the Pacific County wreckmaster was Joseph McKean. It was the wreckmaster's duty to assume charge of any marine wreck after it had been abandoned and to save all of it that was possible for the benefit of the owners. He was charged with protecting wrecks and their cargoes from the "seagulls," a local term that referred to people who helped themselves to treasures that littered the beach after a shipwreck. The wreckmaster was allowed a salvage of 10 percent and was required to file a bond of $2,000. This office no longer appeared on the ballot after 1914.

Wood had made arrangements with the owners of the tug *Daring* of Astoria to be there at the time of the schooner's refloating so that she could be towed safely to port. Everything went according to schedule, except that the tug never showed up.

Many years later, in a memoir called *My Reminiscences In and Around Oysterville*, Clyde Winslow, former Peninsula resident, wrote:

> *Not so successful were efforts to take off the* Solano. *One night, just a day or so before the scheduled attempt to pull her free, a telegram came from the tug company stating they would not be able to get a tug offshore at the critical time necessary for the job. A boy pal, Everette Smith and I, had the assignment that black night to carry that telegram across the Peninsula and out to the captain on the* Solano, *waiting there with his picked crew for the recovery attempt. I no longer remember the reason given for the tug's delay, but I shall never forget the full range and firepower of a sea captain's vocabulary when he grasped the significance of that telegram. Certainly, for me, it opened new vistas of expression. Yet the crew, sitting in the cabin, went right on playing cards without the blink of an eye. However, it was very easy to understand the*

Even as the *Solano* drowned in the accreting sands along the ocean shoreline, she was a major attraction for locals and tourists alike. *Courtesy of the Espy Family Archives.*

frustration of this particular captain. He stood to gain much by taking off the big 4-master, yet lost, as it proved, this last chance for success with the unfortunate Solano.

As the *Solano* wallowed helplessly, a strong south wind whipped up an angry surf. Hour by hour, the breakers mounted until the hapless ship was driven back onto the beach with tremendous force. All further attempts to save the ship were abandoned, and in the subsequent litigation, Wood was awarded half of the appraised value of the schooner, less half the tugboat rate that had been agreed on.

For years, the *Solano* sat forlornly on the beach just south of Oysterville, a landlocked curiosity gradually being swallowed by drifting sands—one of the more interesting sights to show beach visitors. In 1914, my fifteen-year-old aunt, Medora Espy, alluded to one of her own cherished memories of a previous visit to the wreck, apparently with her friend Herbert Davis:

We walked out to the beach and down the beach to the Solano *in the pouring rain. Examined the familiar old H.D. + M.E. Poor old Herbie. I wish I hadn't been so good.*

DROWNING IN SAND

The gale-force winds and driving rains of winter, in combination with the ravages caused by souvenir hunters, diminished the *Solano*'s superstructure bit by bit, and within a few years, she began to drown in the sand. As the old wreck languished, her hull would disappear and rise up and then disappear anew. People began to refer to her as the ghost ship and, by the mid-1920s, thought she had disappeared for good as the sands grew ever deeper along the shoreline.

The vanishing and reappearing *Solano* was only one sign that the beach was changing. The alternate accretion and erosion of sand—but mostly accretion—was (and continues to be) a process familiar to longtime residents of the fragile, mile-wide Peninsula. Even schoolchildren understood that the twenty-eight-mile-long Peninsula was simply a narrow, low-lying sand spit built up from the silt washing down the Columbia and carried north by strong ocean currents off the river's mouth. During the early part of the twentieth century, accretion seemed to be on the upswing.

Engineers and scientists blamed the escalating rate of sand buildup on the north jetty, part of a system of three jetties built at the mouth of the Columbia between 1885 and 1939. They were constructed in an effort to provide safe transit between the Pacific Ocean and the Columbia River by stabilizing the navigation channel as well as minimizing its maintenance. Though the Peninsula had been gradually growing for almost five thousand years, the accretion process increased alarmingly with the completion of the north jetty at Cape Disappointment.

The clearest example was in the town of Long Beach, where the high-tide line seemed to move steadily toward the west. Boulevard, once the most westerly street in town, was now a good distance from the surf. No longer were drift logs washing up into the street during the high tides of December. The beach was broadening, no doubt about it, and north of Ocean Park, it seemed that the *Solano* had finally been buried forever.

GHOSTLY REAPPEARANCE

In 1933, however, the sands moved drastically and the hull again became visible. For the next four decades, the slowly disintegrating ship held its ground tenaciously. As the years passed, the wooden hull bleached white, and the barnacles seemed to completely envelop her old bones; her appearance became more and more ghostly. By the 1950s, she was considered unsafe to walk on, but the deep tide pools below the rotting deck harbored Dungeness crabs, there for the taking by enterprising locals, armed only with garden rakes and buckets.

Youngsters, especially, found the old wreck irresistible. Gary Whitlow, who grew up in Oysterville, still recounts some of his escapades: "I remember Dick and Don Robertson and me doing some fun and crazy things like hiking to the beach to fish. We would get up on the old shipwreck *Solano* and wait until the water came in enough for fishing. Then we would have to stay until the tide went out enough to get back off. Some days, we were stuck out there a long time. Mom never knew about those trips, and it was probably a good thing."

In the mid-1960s, the wreck disappeared again, and as the years have gone by, people have begun to forget its exact location. The dunes continue to shift and grow, and the once familiar landmarks have changed. "Just how far up on the beach was it, anyway? Do you remember?" people ask one

As the old wreck weathered white and barnacles encrusted its remains, the *Solano*'s ghostly appearance became a poignant reminder of days gone by. *Courtesy of the Columbia Pacific Heritage Museum.*

another. Newcomers to the Peninsula are amazed to learn that it ever existed and that the cars on the Ocean Beach Highway might actually be driving right over the bones of the old ship.*

The wreck has been the subject of photographs and paintings and even inspired a book by author Walker A. Tompkins (1909–1988). His affection for the Peninsula stemmed from many adventure-filled summer vacations spent with his uncle, Guy Allison of Ocean Park. Tompkins often wrote his Peninsula friends into his books, and in his 1960 novel, *C.Q. Ghost Ship*, the *Solano* had a starring role.

---

* Driving on the beach is a Peninsula tradition that goes back to the days of horses and stagecoaches when it was the only north–south thruway from Ilwaco to Oysterville. Officially called the Ocean Beach Highway, the Long Beach Peninsula shoreline is part of the state's seashore conservation area that runs up the entire coast of Washington. Driving regulations on the beach are strictly enforced.

5

THE MAN UPSTAIRS AT THE SHELBURNE

When a visiting psychic asked David Campiche if he would like the ghost to leave the Shelburne Inn, there was no hesitation on his part. "Yes," he said. "That was a while back, and it seems to have worked. The man upstairs is gone."

David, who has owned the Shelburne since 1977, had put up with that ghost almost from day one of his proprietorship. "I think he made himself known within the first week that we had the inn," he remembers. "We were doing some major renovations and repairs. Workmen were coming in and out, and we were all busy in the dining room area when we heard someone going up the stairs.

"My first reaction was a feeling of annoyance. I thought that a visitor or curiosity-seeker could at least have had the courtesy to ask permission to look around. Then we heard him walking quite loudly above us, way up on the third floor, so I went up to have a look. There was no one there—no evidence that anyone had been up there at all. It was our first inkling that perhaps we had a ghost."

In the years that followed, that inkling grew to an absolute certainty. Although neither David nor his wife, Laurie Andersen, ever saw the ghost themselves, many an overnight guest did. David recalls one woman who said that she had met an elderly gentleman in the upstairs hall who requested that she sit at Table 9 in the dining room so that he could stand at the top of the stairs and watch her eat.

Located in Seaview, the Shelburne Inn (until 1977, called the Shelburne Hotel) is the longest continuously operating hostelry in Washington State. *Photo by Sydney Stevens.*

Table 9 at the bottom of the back stairway was where the ghost wanted the guest at the Shelburne Inn to sit for dinner. *Photo by Sydney Stevens.*

"She complied," says David, "and we assumed he was watching her, though he did not show himself to any of us or, for that matter, to her."

David's own encounters with the ghost were never visual. Most often, he would be aware of an icy, dense patch of air in the upstairs hallway that joins the two buildings that make up the inn.

"That's also the area where we frequently heard noises that we could not explain," he continues, "both in the hallway and on the upper floors of the northernmost building. That's the older of the two buildings, so in a way, it made sense."

Built in 1896

That first portion of the inn, a two-and-a-half-story wood-frame structure, was built in 1896 as a hotel and boardinghouse. It was located toward the

Built in 1896 and later moved across the street to its present location, this two-and-a-half-story hotel was the beginning of the historic Shelburne Inn. *Courtesy of the Faye Beaver Collection, Pacific County Historical Society.*

south end of the parking lot on the block where Sid's Market* now stands and was built with lumber that was milled in South Bend, barged to Nahcotta and transported to Seaview by the Ilwaco Railroad.

The building had fourteen rooms for permanent and summer boarders and, in addition, was spacious enough to accommodate builder Charles L. Beaver's family, which included his wife, Inez, and their two children—Harold, born in 1892, and Faye, born in 1894. Charles named the hotel the Shelburne after a grand hotel in Dublin, Ireland, and he put his wife in charge of running it.

In later years, Faye often spoke of her memories of life at the hotel, particularly of her mother's wonderful meals that kept guests coming back to Seaview year after year to stay for the summer. Inez Beaver's "home cooking" was centered on the seasonal fowl and game of the area

---

* Sid's Market was established in 1953 by Long Beach resident Sid Snyder and his wife, Bette. The grocery store is located at 4401 Pacific Way in Seaview (across from the present-day Shelburne Inn), and local residents have fond memories of Washington's "Senator Sid" coming home at the end of each legislative season to roll up his sleeves and work in his grocery store.

Left: Inez Eugenia Stout Beaver (1860–1930) ran the Shelburne Hotel while her contractor husband, Charles, concentrated on the development of Seaview. *Courtesy of the Pacific County Historical Society.*

Right: Charles Beaver (1865–1943) built the original Shelburne Hotel as well as many of the cottages that remain a central focus of the Seaview community. *Courtesy of the Pacific County Historical Society.*

as well as the clams, crabs, oysters, fish and wild blackberries. "My mother prepared all of the meals from scratch in a kitchen without benefit of refrigeration—not even an icebox—and, of course, on a wood-burning range," Faye remembered.

While Mrs. Beaver was running the hotel, her husband was busy with his own career. Educated as an attorney in Meadville, Pennsylvania, Charles had come to Seaview in 1889 and was admitted to the bar in Washington the next year. However, after a year of practicing law, he decided that a more lucrative career would be the contracting and building business. Many of the historic cottages of the Seaview area were built for summer visitors from Portland under the direction of Charles Beaver.

The North Beach, as the Peninsula was called, was a popular summer destination in the late nineteenth and early twentieth centuries. Families seeking relief from the hot weather of the inland Oregon valleys often spent all summer in the small coastal communities to the north of the Columbia River. They brought with them their dogs and other pets, perhaps even the

At the turn of the last century, the voyage downriver from Portland to Astoria took five and a half hours on the popular *T.J. Potter*. *Courtesy of the Espy Family Archives.*

family cow for milk. It was not unusual for the more affluent vacationers to bring horses and carriages, as well. Except for a week or two of vacation, it was customary for the men to remain at work in the city during the week and to join their families on the weekends.

On Friday evenings, scores of men would hurry to the wharf in Portland to board a riverboat such as the side-wheeler *T.J. Potter* for the five-and-a-half-hour voyage downriver to Astoria. From Astoria, a launch took travelers to Ilwaco (or, later, to Megler), where they would catch the narrow-gauge railroad train for the journey to Seaview or other communities on the North Beach Peninsula. Because weekend trains were mostly filled to capacity with men traveling to and from the beach, they were dubbed the "Papa Trains" or, sometimes, the "Daddy Trains."

The Beavers operated the Shelburne Hotel for ten years and then moved to Portland, selling the business to Timothy and Julia Hoare. The Hoares were restaurateurs, and for the first five years that they owned the Shelburne, they remained in Portland, leasing out their hotel on the North Beach Peninsula. In 1911, they gave up their Portland interests, moved to Seaview and became full-time hotel proprietors.

CROSSING THE STREET

Soon, the hotel was enlarged, though not in the usual manner. JoAnne Risley, granddaughter of Julia and Timothy, remembered, "Across the street from the Shelburne was a piece of property with two houses on it and with room on the lot for a third. Grandpa Hoare bought the property and hired a team of horses to pull the hotel across the street and place it to the north and in line with the other two buildings. A covered passageway was built between each of the buildings, joining them together and resulting in a much larger hotel."

Mr. Hoare, a canny businessman, also made arrangements with the railroad company to have the Shelburne serve as one of the stops along the line. Today, the original Shelburne is still adjoined to the house directly to its south, and several additions have been made to that part of the inn. The third building is no longer there, though no one seems to remember just what happened to it.

Timothy Hoare died in 1921, and from that point until her death in 1939, Julia managed the hotel on her own. "After Grandpa died, Grandma managed both the hotel and the restaurant, which served three meals a day," said granddaughter JoAnne. "She would get up at 5:30 every morning and get the fires going. Everything in those days was with wood—heating the

The Shelburne Hotel, circa 1915. The middle window in the middle building looks out from Room 8, Julia Hoare's room when she was proprietress. *Courtesy of David Campiche and Laurie Anderson, Innkeepers.*

Julia Hoare ran the Shelburne Hotel on her own after her husband's untimely death in 1921. Her grandchildren remembered her as being "very perfect!" *Courtesy of JoAnne Risely.*

hotel, the cook stove, heating water. She worked all day long, and the very last thing she did each evening before retiring was to scrub the drain boards in the kitchen. To me, she was the greatest woman in the world that could do it all with a happy face. I don't remember that she ever went out. She was always at the hotel."

Julia's was Room 8, which was just above the front door. From that vantage point, she could keep an eye on the comings and goings of her guests and of her hired help.

It is Room 8, according to David, in which one of the strangest of the ghostly happenings occurred. "There was a man, a winemaker from California, staying in that room, and he got locked out. In addition to the lock, which required a key (and which he had kept with him), there was a deadbolt on the door, which could only be locked or unlocked from the inside. This man locked his room from the outside with the key, left the hotel for a time, and when he returned, found that, although his key worked fine, the room remained locked from the inside. Someone had thrown the deadbolt!"

In order to open the door, David had to crawl out the window of the room next door, inch his way along the porch roof, jimmy open Room 8's window and crawl inside to unlock the deadbolt.

"What made it even stranger was that this same man had recently had a really ghastly experience with a ghost in California," David said. "I don't remember all the details now, but it involved bloody scratch marks appearing on the walls and moving from ceiling to floor. Needless to say, the experience at the Shelburne, though mild by comparison, shook him up a little. We gave him another room, and all was well. Not long after that, we changed the deadbolt lock situation."

THE GEARHART TO SEAVIEW CONNECTION

If you happen upon the connection between the beginnings of Gearhart, Oregon, and those of Seaview, Washington, the old adage "behind every successful man is a good woman" may come to mind—perhaps with a daughterly twist. It began with Philip Gearhart.

In 1848, Philip Gearhart was thirty-eight years old, married to Margaret Logan, living in Iowa and looking for a change in the sameness of scenery. The Gearharts headed west in an oxen-drawn covered wagon, arriving in Oregon Territory in the early fall.

Leaving his wife and children in Oregon City, Philip headed down the Columbia River by canoe, located a fertile area on the Clatsop Plain south of Astoria and moved his family there. Several years later, Gearhart took out a donation land claim and platted his holdings. By 1863, the family included six children, and they were well established in a town bearing the Gearhart name.

The Gearharts' oldest daughter, Anne, married Jonathan L. Stout, of Unity (now Ilwaco), Washington Territory, on February 16, 1860. Jonathan was to have what could be termed a "checkered career" during his years on the North Beach Peninsula. At various times, he had his own stage line and was a cooper (barrel maker), a justice of the peace and a saloonkeeper.

The year of Anne Gearhart and Jonathan Stout's twentieth wedding anniversary, Jonathan homesteaded 153.5 acres north of Ilwaco, and a year later, he platted his land

Philip Gearhart (1820–1881) and Margaret Logan Gearhart (1812–1899). *Courtesy of the Pacific County Historical Society.*

into dozens of blocks and lots. He named his town site "Sea View" and promoted it as a resort attraction, opening a large hotel, the Seaview House, which quickly became known for its fashionable amenities, including an elegant ballroom.

But then Jonathan's life began to suffer serious reverses. In 1887, the Stouts' twenty-seven-year marriage ended in divorce. Five years later, Stout's hotel was completely destroyed by fire. He died in financial ruin in the mid-1890s.

However, the family tradition of community growth was carried on. The Stouts' daughter, Inez Eugenia, and their son-in-law, Charles Beaver, continued Jonathan's promotion of Seaview and, like Jonathan, built a resort hotel of their own, the Shelburne. Beaver's contracting business was responsible for more than thirty of the Seaview cottages.

Thus, the Beavers completed the interesting progression of land development and building that had continued from father to daughter and son-in-law over three generations and resulted in the establishment of two communities, one on each side of the Columbia River.

Jonathan Stout (1820–1895) and Anne Elizabeth Gearhart Stout (1840–1910). *Courtesy of the Pacific County Historical Society.*

THE PSYCHIC ARRIVES

Over the years the mysterious noises, the cold air in the hallway and occasional unexplained occurrences continued periodically. Then a psychic from Canada checked into the hotel with a group of her disciples, as David refers to them.

"They stayed for several days," he says, "and had a number of meetings or get-togethers in one another's rooms. Perhaps they were holding séances—I'm not sure. Before they left, the psychic came to me and said, 'I know who your ghost is.'

"I was intrigued, as we had not discussed the ghost at all. I didn't realize she knew anything about it. 'He is Charles Beaver,' she said. 'Do you want him to go away?' 'Yes!' I told her. I didn't hesitate in the least."

Four or five days after the psychic and her entourage had left, David received a phone call. "He's gone," she said. "I saw him leave with two angels." Since that time, which David thinks was ten or so years ago, all manifestations of the ghost have ceased.

"If it was Charles Beaver, maybe he was upset that his hotel had been moved across the street. Or maybe he didn't like that it was joined to another house," speculates David. "It is interesting that it was Julia Hoare's room that he locked. Was he locking her out?"

One other ghost, quite different from Charles Beaver, has revealed itself in the Shelburne as well. In Room 5, on the third floor, there was an old settle—a wooden bench with arms and a high back. David remembers a guest—"a big, strong-looking man"—who came down to the lobby, ashen-faced, to report a little girl in a white pinafore sitting on the settle and swinging her legs.

His was the second report about the little girl, so David, who dislikes having anyone in the hotel—guests or staff—feel uncomfortable, removed the settle. The little girl has not been seen since, although two of the Shelburne employees have had another sort of experience in that particular room.

As part of their duties, Jenelle Berry and Sharon Miller sometimes prepare rooms for check-in—placing the plates of complimentary cookies on the dressers and giving the rooms a last-minute look-over. There is a crib in Room 5 with a teddy bear in it, and on separate occasions, each woman has found the bear on the floor, even though, to their knowledge, no one had been in that part of the inn.

Co-worker Angela Pierce, a fairly recent employee of the Shelburne, says, "I'm not susceptible to paranormal phenomena like some people are, but I wish I were. I'm sorry David told the psychic to get Charles Beaver to leave. I would love knowing that he was still around and that I might possibly have an opportunity to meet him!"

6

THE LITTLE GIRL AT THE MANOR

The big red house on Twelfth and South Idaho Streets is a landmark in Long Beach. For more than one hundred years, it has dominated the block on which it stands—an imposing structure that looks as though it has many stories to tell. Oh, if only it could!

During the years from 1978 to 2000, when Gordon Schoewe and Roy Gustafson owned the house, they tried diligently to learn its history. They spent long hours at the courthouse in South Bend with Pacific County historian Larry Weathers searching the records for information, but to no avail. What Gordon and Roy were eventually able to piece together was based mostly on hearsay and the dimming memories of Long Beach old-timers.

The original part of the house, a farmhouse, was constructed about 1893 and sat on the street side of a cleared and partially swampy area. It was situated a few blocks to the south of Henry Harrison Tinker's "Tinkerville," which, a few years earlier, had been recognized as Long Beach by the United States Post Office Department.

To the south and east of the house was the barn, and between the house and barn was a three-story structure with inward-slanting walls. This distinctive building was topped by a windmill and housed a pump. The upper part was equipped to store the water, which supplied house and farm by gravity feed. By the time of Gordon and Roy's residency, the water tower had been moved south and west. The two upper floors had been removed, and it was being used as a garage.

In this early photograph, the barn and water tower are clearly visible behind the Manor, then called the Knoll, in Long Beach. *Courtesy of Gordon Schoewe.*

The inward-slanting walls of the 1980s garage at the Manor were reminders of the building's beginnings as the farm's three-story water tower. *Photo by Sydney Stevens.*

The original house was a simple one—four rooms downstairs and four up. The staircase to the second story was affixed to the outside of the building in back. Placement of the chimney indicates that the kitchen was downstairs toward the rear, with a dining area behind. A living room, a small bedroom and an entry hall completed the downstairs floor plan. Upstairs, there were three or four bedrooms. There was no inside plumbing in those days, so presumably, there was a privy out back.

THE ADDITION

At an early point in the house's history, a sizeable addition was built at its south end. There was a significant difference in the level of the floors where the two portions of the house were joined. This was especially noticeable in the upstairs hallway where a short step up indicated you were leaving the old part.

When Gordon and Roy bought the place, both the upper and lower stories of the addition consisted of many small rooms. These served to underscore speculation that, following its use as a farmhouse, the building served as a hotel for the increasing demands by the Long Beach tourist trade. It was also rumored that the building was a hospital, a home for young girls or, at one time, a house of ill repute. "As far as we were able to find out," says Gordon, "it could have been all of those things at various times.

"We spent our first few years there living in the middle of a construction zone. The roof leaked like a sieve. There were dozens of buckets and pans scattered around the attic to catch the drips. We hired a new roof done and then began renovating the interior ourselves, one room at a time. Roy did the carpentry and heavy work; I painted walls and hung pictures."

They found that the house was constructed of "first quality cedar and fir" with old-fashioned square nails. Occasionally, they discovered a treasure stashed within the walls—an old train schedule (which they gave to the Columbia Pacific Heritage Museum) and, once, a sarsaparilla bottle. There were no substantive clues, however, about the exact year the house was built or by whom.

In the early 1980s, Roy learned that Charles Beaver might have had something to do with the house's construction. Beaver, a local carpenter in the late nineteenth century, was well known for his excellent craftsmanship. Notable among his projects was the Shelburne Inn, built in 1896.

When Roy discovered that I knew Beaver's daughter, he asked for an introduction. He and I spent an interesting afternoon in Faye's charming Ocean Park cottage. Well into her eighties, Faye Beaver was full of colorful memories of early Long Beach and of her talented father. Unfortunately, she did not know if he had had anything to do with the Manor, as Gordon and Roy called the house.

One of the things that Gordon and Roy did know from the time of their purchase was that the house was haunted. No details—like by whom or how the haunting manifested itself—were supplied. During the twenty-two years they lived in the house, the details would become dramatically apparent, not only to Gordon and Roy, but to many of their friends as well.

UPSTAIRS NOISES

It wasn't until their remodeling projects were completed that the two men began to hear noises upstairs. Although they knew there was no one else in the house, up the steep, narrow stairs they would go to check. Never was there anyone there; never was there evidence that anything had moved or fallen; never was there a logical explanation. As time went by, the noises became more defined. Fast, light footsteps, like those a child might make, could clearly be heard. Sometimes it seemed that a small animal was with the child.

"We always had cats, and we were used to cat sounds. The animal we heard was definitely a cat," Gordon says. "In the beginning, we would assume it was our Chessie. But when we glanced around, we'd see Chessie sound asleep on her favorite pillow or sometimes one of us would actually be holding her.

"Upstairs we would go to see if, by chance, some other animal had gotten in. I had visions of a big rat," he laughs, "but we could never find anything. Gradually it got so we simply assumed it was the ghost child's cat. If Chessie heard the same noises we did, she never gave any indication."

They mostly heard the noises while sitting in their living room, which was situated in the addition, directly below the upstairs hallway. That seemed to be a favorite place for the child to run and play. The child seemed most active while guests were present.

Gordon and Roy had been in the house for two or three years when some friends visited them from Hawaii. A group had gathered for dinner,

Roy and Gordon's cat, Chessie, was usually snoozing in plain view when the mysterious upstairs cat was heard running up and down the hallway above. *Courtesy of Gordon Schoewe.*

and all but one of the guests were in the kitchen kibitzing with the chef. When Roy happened to go back into the living room, the one friend who had stayed behind asked, "Who's the little girl? Is she a neighbor?" There was no child in sight.

Apparently, a little girl about five or six years old and dressed all in white had come into the room and stayed just a few seconds. Neither Gordon nor Roy could account for her. She wasn't a neighbor. She didn't belong to any of the assembled guests. No one else had seen her. "It seemed obvious to all of us that something unusual had occurred," says Gordon, "and as we talked it over we were all convinced that the little girl in white must be the nonexistent child we often heard upstairs."

As far as Gordon knows, that was the only time the girl was actually visible to anyone, but it was not the only time that there was physical evidence of her. When Greta McDougall was house- and cat-sitting for Gordon and Roy one summer, she was awakened by the sensation that something had landed on her bed. She had been warned that she might hear unexplained noises, but she was not prepared for this.

"STOP THAT!"

Immediately wide awake, she got up and walked quietly around the upstairs but heard nothing and saw nothing—until she returned to her room. The end of the bed was moving up and down as if a child were bouncing on the bed. Perhaps as a throwback to her own childhood when bed bouncing was not encouraged, she said in a stern voice, "Stop that! Stop right now," and the bouncing stopped.

Greta had one other experience with what folks came to think of as the "naughty little girl." One night, she was awakened by the door on the bedside stand opening and shutting repeatedly. Recounting the experience later, she said it was annoying and somehow felt like it was being done deliberately. Once again, she spoke sternly as though to a misbehaving child, and once again, peace was restored.

Greta's mother, Bev Smith, can clearly recall an experience she had while visiting the house during one of Greta's sojourns as house sitter. "I was seated at the table in the little breakfast nook off the kitchen. I was facing away from the back door when I heard a knock. It was low down on the door, and I remember thinking, rather inanely, that the cat must be knocking to come in. But the cat was already in the house, and besides," she laughs, "cats don't usually knock! We decided that it must be 'her' again!"

Even more alarming than the noises was the smell of smoke. Several times, Gordon and Roy rushed upstairs looking for a possible fire. "We were always cognizant of living in a big wooden house, and fire was a concern. More than once, we would get the strong odor of smoke, and as we frantically searched the house, it seemed that the odor became stronger as we went upstairs. But we never found anything."

When I asked if he or Roy had ever found evidence of a house fire during their remodeling, Gordon said, "Absolutely none. One odd thing happened, though. Once on one of my frantic fire searches, a friend went racing upstairs with me. On our way back down, after finding the usual nothing, he saw an aura up in one corner of the stairwell. I couldn't see a thing. He said it was sort of a gauzy shape resembling a head and shoulders. Then he pulled up his trouser legs and all the hair on his legs was sticking straight out—like from static electricity or like the fur of a cat when it's upset."

"But," Gordon went on, "there was one dreadful story which could possibly have explained the connection between the old house, the little girl and the smoky smell. For a while, John and Val Campiche owned the house just to the north of us. They never lived there, but John seemed

When the invisible little girl and her cat stopped visiting, Roy Gustafson and Gordon Schoewe actually missed them. *Courtesy of Gordon Schoewe.*

to know a bit about the history of the area. He told us that there once was a little girl associated with our property who had died in a fire. My impression from John was that it was a bonfire, perhaps on the beach. I don't know if the child had actually lived in the house or perhaps was related to someone who lived there."

Several years before Gordon and Roy moved from the Manor, the haunting stopped—no more noises from upstairs, no more unexplained smell of smoke. The little girl and her cat were gone. "You know," smiles Gordon, "we almost missed them."

7

THE GHOST OF AUNT FRANCES

The little girls saw Aunt Frances often, though she had "gone to her reward" years before they were born. She visited them at bedtime for as long as they slept upstairs in the old family house. When they moved to a downstairs bedroom, they didn't see her anymore.

"She always appeared in a sort of smoky aura," remembers Sarah "Sally" Sherwood Abernathy. "She never spoke to us or identified herself. We just knew that it was Aunt Frances. She was my mother's next oldest sister and was the only one of her ten siblings who had died by then, so it seemed obvious to us.

"When we would see her, we were always just a little afraid. But not enough to get spooked about it. She would stand in the hallway, just outside our bedroom door. I think that 'her' room was the northeast bedroom right across from ours."

Frances was born in 1909, the ninth child of Maggie and F.L. Sargant. Like many of the Sargant children, Frances went to Portland when she finished school. She lived with Mae, an older sister who, by then, had a family of her own.

"It was Mae's ten-year-old daughter, Dorothy, who found Frances's body," Sarah says. "Frances was in her late twenties, and she had taken rat poison and was terribly bloated, or at least that's what we were told. No one knew why she did it. That was in 1934.

"My sisters and I were born in the 1940s. We could never figure out why Frances's ghost was hanging around our house since she died in Portland.

Sarah "Sally" Sherwood (middle), age seven, with five-year-old twin sisters, Kathy and Suzie, in 1950, about when they were seeing the ghost of Aunt Frances. *Courtesy of Sarah Abernathy.*

Maybe it was because she grew up there on the bay and was happy in those days of her childhood."

Frances's mother and father had come to the North Beach Peninsula in the early 1900s. Her father, after whom she was named, was Francis Lucas Sargant and was born in Warwick, England, in 1856. His wife, Margaret Ann Timmons (Maggie), was somewhat younger, born in Indiana in 1874.

THE BLACK SHEEP*

"I think my grandfather was the black sheep of his family," speculates Sarah. "I know he got an allowance from his father every year. My grandparents were married on Christmas Eve 1895 in Logansport, Indiana, and their first six children were born in Indiana at nearby Lake Cicot. They moved west sometime between the births of Robert Lucas in Indiana in January 1903 and Laura Mae, who was born in Nahcotta in February 1905.

"The house my sisters and I grew up in was the second house on their property on Willapa Bay," Sarah says. "I remember the remains of the first house. It had been built before my grandparents moved there, but their family was too large to fit, arriving with six children as they did and more coming all of the time—every one to two years!

"My grandmother never lost a baby, and none of the children died after birth. Frances was the first to die, and then later, a brother died from a water heater blowing up at the restaurant he worked at in Alaska, sometime in the fifties. That was long after we had begun seeing the ghost of Aunt Frances.

"According to some of the old pictures, the first house remained standing for quite a while. But by the time we came along, all that was left was some lumber and part of the old roof. The house we lived in—the one that the Tom Downer family has now—was built in 1907 or 1908. I was told that three or four men helped my grandfather build it with lumber that was floated over from Long Island. My mother said that part of the house was built from lumber salvaged from the shipwrecked *Alice,* and that was the source of her name, as well."

In the late 1950s, the Sherwood family sold the farm and moved to California—everyone, that is, except for the ghost of Aunt Frances. According to subsequent owners, the ghost stayed with the house—for a while.

---

* Francis Sargant was often referred to as a "remittance man" by his friends and neighbors—a label used partly with a sense of compassion, partly with a feeling of envy and probably never to his face. "Remittance Men" was the term applied to young Englishmen sent off by their families to live in one of the former British colonies or perhaps in the United States. Most were the second or younger sons of aristocratic and wealthy British families whose assets were traditionally passed down to the first son, leaving the other children with little or nothing, and therefore considered to have few prospects of their own.

Maggie and Francis Sargant are pictured here in 1915 with their eleven children. Frances is third from left in the front row. *Courtesy of Sarah Abernathy.*

Taken from southwest of the Sargant farm, this 1918 photograph shows the first and second family houses as well as the barn and several outbuildings. *Courtesy of Tom Downer.*

THE TELEPHONE GAME

Although all of the succeeding reports of the ghost agree in certain respects, each differs in the details. Like the familiar children's game of "telephone," the tale gets tweaked a bit with each retelling.

Marilyn Casey (who now lives immediately to the south of the old Sargant place) and her husband, Max, bought the house in 1968. "I'm not sure how many owners there were between the Sherwoods and us," says Marilyn. "We bought the property from the Ralph McGough family. I think he got a job in the Grays River area, so they had to move."

Stan Sonntag, a teenager at the time, remembers the McGough family very well. "We lived not far from them. He was a teacher, and I think they had been living in Naselle before they came here. Maybe he had been teaching there," recalls Stan. "Anyway, their daughter was still going to Naselle High School. Her name was Kathy. I took her to a dance once.

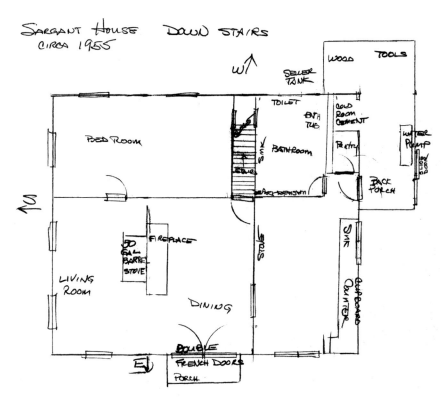

Plan for the first floor of the Sargant House, circa 1940s. *Courtesy of Sarah Abernathy.*

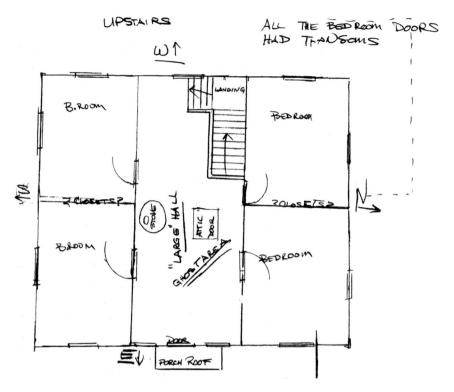

Plan for the second floor of the Sargant House, circa 1940s. *Courtesy of Sarah Abernathy.*

"Not long after that, Mr. McGough got a job in Grays River or Rosburg, maybe as principal of a couple of little schools. They moved away, and the Caseys bought the house. I don't remember ever hearing anything about a ghost at the Sargant place in those days, though."

"At the time we bought the house," says Marilyn, "Max had some horses at the track in Seattle, and we had a small apartment up there. He used the horse trailer to deliver me and the furniture here, but he had to get back to the track right away, so I spent the first few weeks alone in the house.

"The place was pretty run-down, and I set to work scrubbing and painting," she remembers. "When I got the downstairs finished, I started on the upstairs. There were four bedrooms up there. The one in the northeast corner was a pretty little room, which I thought would make a nice guest bedroom.

"Every time I went into that room, I noticed a strange scent, sort of like the fragrance of flowers. And, although I would close the door each time I left, it was always open six or eight inches when I went back up there. It was strange. I was sleeping in the downstairs bedroom, and soon I began hearing footsteps overhead. Someone seemed to be walking in that northeast bedroom and out into the hall during the night. I knew there was no one up there. I didn't even go look. I had a .22 pistol in the drawer by my bed so I felt pretty safe. Somehow, I just knew it was a ghost and not a scary one, either."

"MARILYN, SOMEONE IS UPSTAIRS..."

"It was a while before my husband was able to get away from the track for a few days. The first night he spent in the house, he woke me up saying, 'Marilyn, someone is upstairs.' 'Oh, that's just the ghost,' I told him. But he took the pistol and went up to take a look. He didn't find anything, of course, though he was concerned about that one bedroom door being open."

Later, Marilyn's mother came to housesit for a few weeks so that Marilyn could join Max in Seattle. "She called me the first night, and I knew right away what was bothering her. 'Where's the gun?' she asked. I had taken it with me, so I just told her not to worry. 'You won't need the gun. It's only the ghost,' I said.

"I was curious who the ghost might be. I asked some of the neighbors who had been around for a while if anyone had ever died in the house. I was told that there had been a young girl—a teenager—who had died there. They said that she had a boyfriend who had left her unexpectedly and she committed suicide. In that northeast bedroom.

"I often went upstairs to sit in the southeast bedroom to read. I loved looking out the windows from that room. There was an old apple tree outside the east window, and a big barn owl would visit it now and then.

"Once while I was up there, I heard footsteps and then the mattress sank down like someone was sitting beside me," says Marilyn. "I've often cursed myself for not speaking to her that day or even looking over at her. For some reason I just kept staring out the window.

"We only had one unpleasant experience with the ghost. My husband's niece had come to visit, and even though I had told her about the ghost, she chose that northeast bedroom. She was the fearless type."

FEELING OF MENACE

"At bedtime, she went in and turned down the bedding but, at the last minute, decided to sleep in the room across the hall instead. My husband woke up during the night and said, 'What's the matter with that ghost?' She had come downstairs and was outside our bedroom. My husband was sure she was upset. There was an angry, warning feeling—a menace in the doorway. 'Her' bed was still turned down, though not slept in. I think that's what upset her. It's the only time she ever came downstairs, like she wanted us to know that her room should be left alone. After a few years, we didn't hear her anymore. The fragrance was gone, too. She just sort of faded away."

"I think she went home with me," says Ron Cox of Ocean Park. "I really do. We never had any strange stuff happening at our house until after I worked on that old house for the Downers back in the 1980s."

According to Ron, he did some remodeling work on the house after the Downers purchased it in 1982. "The first time I was aware of something odd was at the end of one workday when I was taking some tools back to the old chicken shed. That was where I kept all my tools, but when I went in there that evening, my toolbox was gone. I looked all around—even went back to the house to see if I'd taken it there and forgotten. No toolbox."

"So I went over to Jack's Country Store and asked Tom if he had borrowed my tools for any reason. Nope. I went back to check around again, and something told me to go into that shed one more time, even though I'd already checked it carefully. And there it was! Right in the middle of the

At Jack's Country Store, proprietor Tom Downer had no answers about what had happened to Ron Cox's missing toolbox. *Photo by Sydney Stevens.*

floor. There was no way I could have missed it if it had been there before. Nothing was disturbed or missing. It was just sitting there!

"Sometime later, someone told me there was supposed to be a ghost in the house in the northeast bedroom upstairs," remembers Ron, "but I never saw or heard anything—just that thing with my tools in the shed. I was still working there, though, when strange things began happening here at my own house! I had three car titles that I kept right on top in a certain desk drawer. I needed them for something, but when I looked for them, they weren't there. I tore the place apart, but I couldn't find them anywhere. A few days later, I decided to have one more look. And there they were, right on top in the drawer where they were supposed to be."

A Gray Thing

According to Ron, on different occasions, both his daughter and his grandson have seen the ghost. "They described her as a 'gray thing,' and my daughter said to it, 'Who are you and what do you want?' But there was no answer.

"The way the story was told to me," says Ron, "is that it's the ghost of the daughter of a family who lived in that old house. It was a long time ago, maybe in the late 1800s or early 1900s. The story is that she got pregnant and when she confronted her boyfriend, he took off for Portland. She committed suicide by taking rat poison right in that northeast bedroom. But she never showed herself or did anything when I was working on the house except for 'borrowing' my tools. And Tom says they've never seen her, either. I'm pretty sure that's because she's over at my place now."

Ron describes her antics as those of a teenager. "She likes to borrow the car keys. They disappear for a few days and then they are back where we usually keep them. She's not mean—she's just sort of mischievous or a little irresponsible like a typical eighteen-year-old. I think she's lonely. I sure wish I knew her name. I think maybe it's Katherine."

That the ghost is a young woman, the northeast bedroom in the old Sargant house was hers and she cut short her own life—these all seem to be parts of the story that are agreed upon. Exactly who she was and the circumstances of her death remain shrouded in mystery.

"I wish I'd asked my mom about her," says Sarah. "But we were just little kids. We were always having experiences that we didn't talk to adults about. Those questions only seem important later—you know, after it's too late."

8

"YOU CAN CALL ME UNCLE WILL..."

He told us his name was Will Cox and that he had been killed by a knife. We never could keep sharp knives in the house. They would just disappear," says Jennifer Lonergan of Ocean Park.

"He didn't take table knives or butter knives. Just kitchen knives with sharp points and sharp blades. They are the ones that would vanish. Once, my mom found a missing knife in the garden months after it had disappeared. But usually they never showed up again."

Jennifer was nine or ten years old and living in the Little Red Cottage in Oysterville with her folks, Ruby and Pete Heckes, when Will Cox made himself known. It was 1966.

"The house was small, as it still is. During the time we lived there, you walked directly into the main room, which was a kitchen/dining/living room area. Straight in front of you was a little hallway with a bedroom at each side and a bathroom in the middle. That was it.

"We had a curio cabinet right by the front door. I was always a little worried that I would bump into it and cause damage to the old bottles and keepsakes that were in it. One night there was a huge crash that woke us all up. We all had the same thought and rushed into the living room expecting to see that curio cabinet and its contents totally smashed. But not a thing was broken or even disturbed."

That event prompted the family to find out what was going on. They went to the Ouija board for help. "That's when we found out who he was," says Jennifer. "He said his name was Will Cox and that he had been

Built in 1857 (or 1863?), the Little Red Cottage is the oldest surviving structure in Oysterville—perhaps a likely location for ghostly visits. *Photo by Sydney Stevens.*

This familiar type of "talking board" is what Jennifer and her family used to converse with Uncle Will. *Courtesy of the Espy Family Archives.*

killed by a knife. According to him, he was taking all of our knives away to keep me safe."

"He said, 'You can call me Uncle Will.' He said he was watching over me. Or at least that was the message he sent on the Ouija board. He sent us quite a few messages, but we never did see him, even though I kept asking. He told me that I wasn't 'ready.' The last time I asked, we were all sitting at the table with the Ouija board and there was a really loud *thump*. I jumped straight out of my chair. 'See, I told you that you weren't ready!' he said."

WHO WAS WILL COX?

According to Jennifer, Will Cox continued to make himself known to the family, even after they had moved. "In fact," she says, "we moved twice before Pete's house on the bay was finished—once to the little Wachsmuth house on the corner about a block north of the red cottage, and a year or so later to a house a little south of Oysterville near Vance and Imogene Tartar's place. In both those moves, Will Cox stuck to us. When we finally moved to the bay house, he stopped bothering us."

The subjects of this early photograph, taken in front of Oysterville's Swan Restaurant, remain unidentified. Could one of them be the mysterious Will Cox? *Courtesy of the Espy Family Archives.*

So, who was Will Cox? There is no record of a Will Cox, a William Cox or even a Wilcox ever having lived in Oysterville—not in the census reports and not in the cemetery records. Nor, as far as early records expert Sandy Tellvik can determine, was there anyone by that name in any of the other communities on the Peninsula.

Given that the red cottage is the oldest structure in Oysterville, perhaps the oldest on the Peninsula, the building is a well-qualified candidate for a resident ghost. It was built during Oysterville's boomtown years, when the native oysters of Shoalwater Bay dominated the "Shoalwater Trade" between Washington Territory and San Francisco. Among the men involved in building the structure, there were certainly those who would be concerned about the welfare of children—willing to "watch out" for young Jennifer. But none named Will Cox.

According to the 1860 census, the inhabitants of House 86 in Oysterville were Captain J.W. Munson, age thirty-nine; Sophia Kimball Munson, age nineteen; Frederick Munson, five months old; Byron Kimball, age twenty-three; and James Johnson, age twenty-four. Nathan Kimball, brother to Sophia and Byron, lived a block or so to the north at the Stevens Hotel. Across the street lived an older sister, Susan Kimball Wirt.

MASSACRE SURVIVORS

Sophia Munson, her sister, Susan, and their brothers, Byron and Nathan, were survivors of the 1847 Whitman Massacre at Waiilatpu near the site of today's Walla Walla. Their father had been killed during that bloody attack, and the four children (Sophia, six; Byron, eight; Nathan, ten; and Susan, fourteen), along with their mother and infant sister, had been held prisoner for more than a month until a rescue party negotiated their release. Not many could claim a more compelling personal reason for feeling protective toward a child, yet there was not a man named Will among them.

It is not clear whether House 86 where Sophia and Byron were living in 1860 was the building now known as the "Little Red Cottage." What is clear is that the cottage (for many years called "Munson's Store") was built by Captain Munson and the Kimball brothers, perhaps as early as 1857 but maybe not until 1863. Records at the Pacific County Historical Society are uncertain as to date but indicate that the men were all carpenters, possibly trained as boat-builders. The cottage is built and braced like a ship.

Captain Munson arrived in Oysterville in 1857 and married two years later. The following year, Sophia invited her friend Bethenia Owens to come to Oysterville for a visit. The two young women had known one another since Sophia's post-rescue years growing up on Clatsop Plains in Oregon.

In later years, Bethenia said, "I told Mrs. Munson of my great anxiety for an education, and she immediately said: 'Why not, then, stay with me, and go to school; we have a good school here, and I should like so much to have you with me.'"

Bethenia took her up on the offer, and the start she got in Oysterville inspired Bethenia to continue her education. She went on to become Oregon's first female doctor, the well-respected Dr. Bethenia Owens-Adair. In her autobiography, she spoke highly of Captain Munson, and though the autobiography does not further the quest for Will Cox, it gives an admiring portrait of one of the cottage's earliest inhabitants.

BETHENIA'S STORY

Mr. Munson might well be called a "diamond in the rough." He had a big heart, a hilarious, jovial disposition, and loved good company and a good social time.

He was a tall, broad-shouldered, powerfully-built man, with a large, square head. He was a natural musician, and loved the violin on which he could play by the hour, day or night, and never tire. I have heard him say, "I believe I could play in my sleep if I tried." I have seen him play and laugh and talk at the same time, never missing a note or losing time or expression.

Dancing was the popular amusement in those early times, and to dance well was an admired accomplishment. For this good music was essential, and if Mr. Munson could be secured for any party its success was assured.

I have seen him, when the dancing set became entangled, raise himself to his full, commanding height, dropping his violin by his side, with his hand holding his bow uplifted, with a broad smile on his face, and a vigorous stamp of his foot, call out in a stentorian voice, "Hold on, now, and get straightened out!" Then, with an energetic and artistic stroke of his bow, accompanied by another stamp of his foot, he would start them on again

If they failed a second time, he would exclaim: "Here, now, just change off! Some of you old dancers come over here and help these new

THE WHITMAN MASSACRE, 1847

From the vantage point of more than 150 years, the tragedy at Waiilatpu on November 29, 1847, appears to be the inevitable result of a clash between cultures—in retrospect avoidable but at the time unforeseen. On that fateful Monday and the days following, fourteen white settlers and missionaries died at the hands of Cayuse and Umatilla tribal members. Fifty-four others were taken prisoner. The incident led to the Cayuse War, which in turn resulted in many more deaths to the Indians themselves.

Waiilatpu was a Christian mission on the Walla Walla River operated by Dr. Marcus Whitman (1802–1847) and his wife, Narcissa Prentiss Whitman (1808–1847). Located about six miles from Fort Walla Walla and the present-day town of the same name, the mission served as an important rest stop for immigrants on the Oregon Trail.

Marcus and Narcissa were both from upstate New York. They made the arduous journey west in 1836 and were determined to bring Christianity to the Cayuse Indians at Waiilatpu, laboring hard to make the mission a success. Marcus held church services, practiced medicine and constructed numerous buildings; Narcissa ran their household, assisted in the religious services and taught at the mission school.

Yet from the beginning, the difference in white and Indian cultures laid the groundwork for misunderstandings and conflict. Shortly after selecting a site for his mission, Dr. Whitman prevailed upon the Indian men to assist him with house-building, which they agreed to do, even though they considered putting up lodges to be women's work. They were perplexed that Mrs. Whitman did not help and could not understand why Dr. Whitman did many of the menial tasks expected of a wife. These differences caused the missionaries to lose stature in the eyes of the Indians.

Not only were accepted social and political values at issue, but simple concepts of privacy and hospitality were confusing to both sides. The Indians did not understand why they were not welcome in the Whitmans' home—not to eat and, even worse, not to worship. Too, they were scolded for looking through the windows, even though they had helped build the house. Yet, though the Whitmans did not extend hospitality to the ones they called their "children," they were welcoming to travelers passing through.

The efforts of the Whitmans to Christianize the Indians did not go well. As the missionaries became more and more discouraged by the failure of their efforts, they spent a greater portion of their time in assisting American settlers. To add insult to injury, the increasing number of whites coming into Oregon brought with them numerous diseases— illnesses that ravaged the Indians. The aid offered by the Whitmans to those suffering in the wagon trains magnified the alienation between the Indians and the missionaries.

In late 1847, when an epidemic of measles struck nearby whites and Cayuse alike, the Whitmans ministered to both. However, most of the white children (who had some basic immunity to the disease) lived, while about half of the Cayuse, including nearly all their children, died.

On November 29, 1847, several Cayuse, under the leadership of their chief, took revenge for the deaths, which were perceived by them as treachery. The ensuing slaughter, which would become known as the Whitman Massacre, and the imprisonment of the survivors outraged white settlers in the Oregon Territory, and in the Willamette Valley, a force of volunteers was raised to deal with the problem.

A subsequent white militia attack on a band of uninvolved Cayuse escalated the conflict into a war, which went very poorly for the Indians. Finally, two years after the massacre, Chief Tiloukaikt and several others involved in the attack on the mission voluntarily surrendered in an effort to avoid the destruction of the entire tribe. On June 3, 1850, they were publicly hanged.

Eventually, weakened by disease and subjected to continued white raids, the remaining members of the Cayuse tribe were removed to the Umatilla Reservation in Oregon where they were absorbed among other tribes, ultimately losing their own identity and language. Thus, the Whitmans' well-meaning efforts not only resulted in their own deaths but also led to the end of the Cayuse as an independent people.

The incident remains controversial to this day—the Whitmans are regarded by some as pioneer heroes and martyrs; others see them as white settlers who unjustly intruded on the Native Americans by imposing their own religious and lifestyle values.

ones out!" In the end he was sure to bring order out of confusion, and in such a joyous, hearty way that everyone laughed at his own mistakes and no one felt hurt.

He was as much a captain in the ballroom as on board his steamboat. He was a most excellent mechanic and a fine machinist, and he could make anything, from a steamboat to a violin. Like the traditional busy bee, he was never idle…

Mr. Munson manufactured a number of violins, some of which were valuable. One of these he made from a piece of hardwood which he found several feet below the surface while digging a drain in a swamp near the lighthouse. No hardwood grows anywhere near that vicinity, and this fragment must have drifted ashore long years before and had been covered with [the] debris, it may be, of a century. Thus with his skillful hands and fertile brain he was able to bring sweet music from the very bowels of the earth with which to charm the senses and make glad the heart. He did his best, and did it well. Who can do more?

OYSTERVILLE'S FIRST COURTHOUSE

Various accounts indicate that Captain Munson left Oysterville in 1863 and was appointed light keeper at Cape Disappointment in 1865. Pacific County rented his cottage in Oysterville to be used as a courthouse in 1866. Three years later, the county purchased the building, probably from Munson, although one report said that the county bought it from Andrew Wirt, Susan Kimball Wirt's stepson. The building, the first Pacific County courthouse purchased with public funds, continued to be used for county business until a large, two-story courthouse was built in 1875.

From that point forward, owners and renters were many, but only one other tenant ever reported any ghost activity. The late Ken Driscoll of Ocean Park took up residence in the cottage for a time shortly after the Heckes family lived there. He later told Pete Heckes that, on several occasions, he was visited during the wee hours by someone who would pull the quilts off his bed.

"There would be a struggle," Pete remembers Ken telling him. "I would tug, and he would tug. But there never was anyone to actually see."

Was it the same Will Cox? The taking of something that was not rightfully his (as with the knives in Ruby's kitchen) sounds a bit like Cox's "M.O."

Perhaps any records concerning Will Cox were lost during the infamous 1893 kidnapping of the county seat when South Bend raiders ravaged the Oysterville courthouse. *Courtesy of the Espy Family Archives.*

Surely, though, removing Ken's covers on cold winter nights couldn't have been considered protective, even by a ghost.

My uncle, author Willard Espy, owned the cottage for twenty-five years—from the early 1970s through the mid-nineties. Neither he nor his wife, Louise, ever spoke of ghost-like occurrences at the cottage. Willard was as fond of yarns as the next person, and I can't help but think that if Will Cox had made himself known during those years, the story would have been told and retold—probably in one of Willard's many books.

As it stands, however, Will Cox remains an enigma, and the picturesque little red cottage in Oysterville reveals nothing of its spirited past. At least for now.

9
THE MOREHEAD HOUSE MYSTERY; OR THE CASE OF MILLIE AND HER "IT"

According to those who remember her, Millie Sherwood was girlish and flirtatious, had a soft, lilting voice and gave the impression of being dainty and frail. She was about five feet five, very slender, light on her feet and loved to dance. And she was friendly with a ghost. In fact, Millie was so fond of her ghost that she wrote both a book and a poem about it.

> *IT*
> *I have a little IT.*
> *Without a leg IT walks...*
> *It matters not a whit*
> *That IT neither walks nor talks.*
> *We heard steps in a room*
> *But found no human trace;*
> *Now Suzy's steeped in gloom*
> *With a cloud upon her face.*
> *But 'twas the truth I said*
> *When I said no one walked there,*
> *And she muttered, "He's undead,*
> *I heard him walk, I'll swear!"*
> *So now when I can't sleep*
> *And up the stairs I steal*
> *In darkness still and deep*
> *My little IT I feel.*

Sometimes the gooseflesh cold
Slides down my wary back,
But my IT, It is not bold
Or perhaps IT lacks the knack
Of making ITself known
By physical manifestation...
Still when I'm all alone
And have a warm sensation
It's IT...and here IT dwells
And with me walks the floor
When I have sleepless spells,
(It is really quite a bore
To hear ITs footless step
And know that IT's undead
For I'd hoped IT had the pep
To join me in my bed.)
...How cuddly we would be...
Just my little IT and me.

The ghost, Millie's "IT," manifested not long after she and her family moved into the old Morehead house in Nahcotta in 1947. For the nine years prior to that, she and her husband, Eddie, and daughters, Ann "Memi" and Betty, had lived in Oysterville next door to their cannery, the Sherwood Company.

Millie's daughter Ann remembers, "The cannery and house were very close together, and Eddie (my stepdad) attached them by a walkway that led to the kitchen entrance in the backyard. The workers used the kitchen for their lunch break. Eventually, Eddie started bringing cases of canned smoked oysters and smoked oyster spread into the living room for us to label because there was no room in the cannery to do it. Mom and I did most of the labeling. I thought it was fun, and the best part for me was being with her. The labels had a little Robin Hood logo, and I wish I had saved one.

"Right there among the furniture and the big old harpsichord, we sat labeling those cans, and one day, Mom had her fill of it and decided to buy a different house, and the Morehead house happened to be for sale. Eddie didn't want to. Why should he? He had everything he wanted, work and home, all in the same place! Mom always got her way, and so we bought the Morehead house from Johnny Morehead and moved in."

"Of course, I thought my mom was the most beautiful woman in the world," says Ann Anderson of her mother, Millie Sherwood. *Courtesy of Ann Sherwood Anderson.*

The work crew poses in front of the Sherwood Cannery opening house. Eddie and Millie Sherwood stand behind. *Courtesy of Ann Sherwood Anderson.*

Millie loved the house from the get-go. The very first paragraph in her book, *To Know What Dream*, describes her romantic impression of the house:

> *I'll never forget the first time I saw Old Manse. That day as today, heavy dark clouds massed in the sky and glowered down on the vine-shrouded old house; half-hidden from sight of the street, Old Manse sprawled in an untidy bed and brooded impassively among the shaggy cypress trees in the yard.*

Perhaps the Morehead house was not so overgrown as the Old Manse of Millie's book. However, it did sit among Monterey cypress trees, probably planted by John "J.A." Morehead (Johnny Morehead's father) not long after he built the house in 1889.

"Oh, my goodness, yes, the cypress trees were there!" says Ann. "They were in the front yard over in the corner closest to Rutzers'. I sat in the biggest one all the time and read books. Was it stickery? Yes! But I just wanted to sit in a tree. There were trees on the other side, by Ogden's, but I don't know what they were except for one beautiful purple wisteria. In Mom's attempt

Left: The artwork on Millie's *To Know What Dream* is dark and brooding. The book, now out of print, is based on her experiences in the Morehead house. *Courtesy of Ann Sherwood Anderson.*

Below: The Morehead house when Ann Sherwood Anderson lived there and how she pictures the Old Manse of her mother's story. *Courtesy of Ann Sherwood Anderson.*

at writing a book about the Ozarks, she named her little heroine Wistful Wisteria. Also in the back was an apple tree. I don't know what kind, but those old gnarly apples were the best I have ever eaten.

"When we first moved into the house, the front door opened to the stairway and a narrow hallway. A door led to the right into the living room. Mom didn't like that dark hallway and thought it would be nice to enlarge the living room, so she asked Eddie to tear down that hall wall.

"He didn't want to and so put off doing it until one day, he came home and Mom had taken an axe to it. She always found a method to get her own way! So, he was forced into tearing it down, and the wall of the stairway he covered in knotty pine. He put black tile on the floor. I remember that because squares of it kept popping up. It did *not* make for a cozy room."

Millie's ghost was of the poltergeist variety. Items seemed to move from one place to another and would sometimes break on the journey.

"I remember an ashtray that broke in half. One part was on the radio and the other part was somewhere else in the room," says Ann. "And one time, the sheers behind the draperies in the living room were mysteriously torn. They looked just like a cat had gotten claws stuck in them and shredded them, just around the bottom. Trouble is, we had no cat. What do you make of that?

"My mother enjoyed all of this. She was a dramatic person with a lively imagination, and I think she must have been lonely because during that period of time, Eddie was working long hours at the cannery. And she really loved that house!" This paragraph from her book tells how she felt:

> *For a moment I stood alone in the dim quiet of the empty hall; the house seemed to come to life around me; I could feel the friendly embrace of walls, a welcome as warm as the greeting between friends. It is so still here, I thought, so peaceful. I have come home at last, Old Manse. I am here with you where I belong.*

Ann was thirteen and her sister, Betty, was seventeen when the family moved into the house. "I never had any experiences with IT except through Mom. She put things into my head, but they didn't last long because I was too busy doing school and normal things. I don't think Betty ever had ghost experiences, either. Eddie was too down to earth, where everything was cut and dried.

"We all just considered IT Mom's personal ghost. I think we accepted her explanations of all the things she attributed to the ghost, but I don't remember that the rest of us had any firsthand experiences with IT. Oh! Except I do remember that once something of mine disappeared in that house!

"I had saved my money and bought my mother a huge heart-shaped box of chocolates for Valentine's Day. I put it on the top shelf of my closet in my bedroom. On Valentine's Day, I went to get it and it was gone! Not just chocolates gone out of it, but box and all. I never had a clue who took it, or if someone did, how did she get into my room and back out the front door and down the street with no one seeing her? I say 'her' because I didn't have *boys* in my bedroom!"

Sandra Stone Tellvik, Ann's cousin, also recalls hearing about the ghost in the house. "I remember one time being at the house standing on the bottom of the stairs and Memi pointed to a closed door at the top of the stairs, saying something like, 'That's where the ghost is supposed to be.' That's the extent of my memory about the ghost."

As for the other kids who lived nearby in those days—Phil and Lou Stamp, Billy Winn—none remembers hearing about the ghost. "I think that's probably because those of us in the family just considered it Mom's own private ghost," says Ann. "We didn't talk about IT much.

"Also, I do remember a second ghost. It was a woman, and she lived in the attic. I knew there was a reason why Mom didn't like me to go up there. Remember the widow's walk at the very top of the house? We used to hear her footsteps, pacing and pacing on the walk. Mom explained to me that the ghost was probably waiting for her husband to come home from the sea. Were any of the Moreheads sea-goers I wonder? I remember hearing the footsteps, but Mom also heard her crying. I didn't hear that. Do you think it was one of the Morehead women, waiting for her husband to come home?"

According to Dorothy Trondsen Williams, granddaughter of John and Lizzie Brown Morehead, none of the Moreheads were seagoing men, but Lizzie's father, John Brown, was. Dorothy gave an account of her pioneering ancestors in *They Remembered, Book III*, written in 1992 by Charlotte and Edgar Davis:

> *Brown had gone to sea at the age of 12 from his home in Bergen, Norway and by the age of 17 had rounded Cape Horn three times and twice circumnavigated the earth. This made him a very experienced seaman by the time he arrived in the United States in 1859…[In 1874] he was awarded the mail contract and consequently moved his*

J.A. AND LIZZIE MOREHEAD: NAHCOTTA PIONEERS

When Lewis Alfred Loomis hit the brakes on his narrow-gauge railroad's forward progress in 1889 and made Nahcotta the terminus for his Ilwaco Railroad and Navigation Company operation, young J.A. Morehead (always called "J.A.," never John) clearly saw where his own future lay. It was not in Oysterville where, for the past four years, he had labored as storekeeper and postmaster and where he, along with others, had thought the railroad would terminate. His future was in the newly platted town of Nahcotta just four miles to the south.

Perhaps, too, J.A. felt a degree of loyalty to Mr. Loomis. After all, he had worked as a stage driver for Loomis from 1882 to 1885 and would later write a colorful account of those days of driving on the "weather beach," as the shore of the ocean beach was called. Additionally, Loomis had backed J.A. when he first entered the store business in 1885—the same year that he married Lizzie Brown.

In 1889, J.A. and Lizzie built their substantial home in Nahcotta and relocated their business, Morehead and Company General Merchandise, just to the south of the new railroad. J.A. ran the store

In 1900, the Morehead store dominated the main street in downtown Nahcotta. *Courtesy of the Columbia Pacific Heritage Museum.*

Torvald Trondsen and Henry Brown ready their sign that will replace "Morehead & Co." on Nahcotta's General Merchandise Company store. *Courtesy of Dorothy Trondsen Williams.*

for twenty-six years and carried items as diverse as dry goods, groceries, paints, shoes, hardware, medicine, in-season fruits and vegetables, fresh meat, salmon, crabs, ammunition and glassware. Within ten years, a branch store was built in Ocean Park and was managed by E.J. Sprague.

J.A. and Lizzie had three children—Enola, Bess and Johnny—whose schoolmates included the Wiegardts and children of other Nahcotta pioneers. Lizzie managed the household and was supportive of her husband's many and varied interests.

In addition to his store duties, J.A. found time to lead a life of active public service. He served a total of fourteen years as Pacific County commissioner. He helped organize the Pacific State Bank in South Bend, was president of the Pacific County Pioneer Association and created many of the displays of Pacific County products at the state fairs. J.A. raised cattle and grew peas and daffodils. In his later years, he bought property at the north end of Nahcotta and devoted himself to creating Morehead Park and Camp Morehead. He also donated land to be used as the right-of-way for the county dock "for the good of the public forever."

In 1914, Torvald Trondsen and Henry Brown bought out Morehead and Company. In a way, the business stayed in the family, as Torvald would marry J.A. and Lizzie's daughter, Bess, in 1921, and Henry was Lizzie Morehead's brother. Eventually, both the Nahcotta and Ocean Park stores were sold out of the family, but the Morehead mercantile legacy still continues through Jack's Country Store in Ocean Park, the present-day direct descendant of Morehead and Company General Merchandise.

In the early twentieth century, the oyster boats of Shoalwater Bay would have been a common sight from the Moreheads' widow's walk. *Courtesy of the Espy Family Archives.*

family on to Oysterville. He delivered the mail to all the settlements on the Bay, first using a plunger and after two years the steamers Garfield *and* Montesano. *He was the first to captain a steamship on Shoalwater Bay.*

One might imagine that John and Lizzie included the widow's walk in their house plans so that Lizzie could keep an eye on her father's progress as he plied the waters of the bay. However, by the year the house was built, Captain Brown was no longer traveling those waters on a regular basis. By then, he was serving as keeper of the Shoalwater Bay Lifesaving Station at North Cove, a position he acquired in 1884 and was to hold until his death in 1910.

"I really don't know why they built that widow's walk," muses Dorothy. "I imagine it was just the fashion in those years."

By the time Dorothy remembers the Morehead house in the late 1920s or early 1930s, the railing that delineated the widow's walk was gone. "I was quite surprised to see it there in the early photographs. I didn't realize there had been one at all."

THE EVOLUTION OF A HOUSE

The earliest known photograph of the J.A. Morehead House in Nahcotta was taken in 1890, shortly after it was built. The scalloped-shingle siding, the balcony over the front porch and the wrought-iron fence around the widow's walk on the roof give the otherwise plain building an air of distinction. Two chimneys can be seen toward the back of the roof, and the windmill behind the house is clearly visible.

J.A. Morehead House, 1890. *Courtesy of Columbia Pacific Heritage Museum.*

As the decades have passed, many changes have taken place. Some features have disappeared entirely—the fence around the widow's walk, the door to the balcony over the front porch and, of course, the balcony itself. The two brick chimneys in the back of the house and the windmill are also gone now. Additions have also occurred—the house is now sided with shakes; the northernmost chimney has been replaced with a stovepipe; the porch has been enclosed and incorporated into

J.A. Morehead House, 1947. *Courtesy of Ann Sherwood Anderson.*

J.A. Morehead House, 1960. *Courtesy of Ann Sherwood Anderson.*

J.A. Morehead House, 2008 *Photo by Sydney Stevens.*

an addition to the east and north on the first floor; and a brick chimney rises on the north side of the house.

Even with all the changes, those folks who have lived for any length of time in Nahcotta can tell you exactly which building is the Morehead House. Throughout its slow evolution, the character of the J.A. Morehead House (and perhaps its ghost) has remained unchanged.

"I think Millie just didn't want the kids up there messing around on the roof," laughs Ron Biggs of Oysterville, another of Ann's many cousins. "There's nothing like a little ghost talk to keep kids in line!"

"Perhaps," concedes Ann, "but it actually was a perfect house for a haunting, especially with the spooky attic. If there was a ghost, my mom was just the one to tune in to IT and make it interesting for all the rest of us, too!"

10

A House Fit for a Bride

For more than a century, the elegant white house has stood on the ocean ridge at the north end of Long Beach—a landmark for the generations. Some say the three-story building, capped with a generous widow's walk, resembles a gigantic wedding cake. Only the bride and groom are missing from the top.

The comparison is a good one, for the cottage was completed in 1898 and was presented as a belated wedding gift to Elizabeth Lambert following her marriage to oculist Dr. William Lee Wood in 1894. According to some accounts, the house was built and given to Elizabeth by her father, Joseph Hamilton Lambert. Others have said that the groom himself purchased the land and built the house for his bride.

Whichever beginning it had, the imposing seventeen-room summer place remained the Long Beach home of Elizabeth Lambert Wood for almost seventy years, until her death in 1962. It was built as a vacation home in the days when Portland residents fled the hot summer weather of the interior and came to the North Beach Peninsula to enjoy the cool, misty ocean breezes. Although Mrs. Wood and her family would always have other homes, either in the Portland area or in Oracle, Arizona, the Long Beach house remained a constant in their lives.

The house was known for three unique characteristics: it had the highest viewpoint along the beach, it was closest to the ocean and it was the farthest north—all features that have changed in the ensuing years. Nowadays, there are structures as tall or taller along the beach; the dunes

The Long Beach, Washington house of Elizabeth Lambert Wood has been a landmark for generations. *Courtesy of Candy Glenn.*

have accreted many hundreds of feet, greatly distancing the house from the high-tide line; and mile upon mile of buildings now march northward beyond the distinctive old home. Mrs. Wood's early stationery gave her return address as "Tioga," once a stop to the north of Long Beach along the narrow-gauge railway line—a community that has long since been absorbed by the city of Long Beach.

At the time of construction, high tides came within a few feet of the property's westerly fence line. Lumber was brought onto the beach by the barge load. The barges were floated in on a high tide and then dragged by teams of horses to the building site. One story that persists about the Elizabeth Lambert Wood House is that the builder, whether Mr. Lambert or Dr. Wood, had the house constructed as close as practical to the grounded barges to reduce costs for offloading the lumber.

PIONEER ROOTS

Elizabeth took great pride in her family's pioneer roots in Oregon Territory. In later years, she wrote a short sketch of her life in which she said:

> *My mother's parents, Henry Miller and Mary Shultz Miller crossed the plains in 1853 to Oregon from Fort Wayne, Indiana with my mother, Clementine Mary, then fourteen and the oldest of eight children. In the fall of 1854 she married my father, Joseph Hamilton Lambert of Terre Haute, Indiana, who had arrived by ox-team three years before.*
>
> *He was already established as an experienced fruit man. He, with two other men, had grafted one hundred thousand native stock wild cherry and crabapple with scions brought in wet sand across the plains. On the east bank of the Willamette River, six miles south of Portland, was planted the first commercial orchard in the Oregon country. My grandfather was Oregon's first nurseryman, and planted many of the fine earlier gardens with imported shrubs, trees, and flowers. I remember his giving the first lectures on rose culture in Portland. He was very successful in the outdoor propagation of the camellia, a flowering evergreen.*
>
> *Father continued to experiment with fruit culture and originated the Lambert cherry which is still a well-known commercial variety of sweet cherry that is grown everywhere. In 1892 we moved to Portland where*

Dr. William Lee Wood was a fine horseman. He and Mrs. Wood enjoyed taking long pack trips in the countryside near their Oracle, Arizona home. *Courtesy of Candy Glenn.*

father organized the Citizens' Bank, the second oldest bank in the city. He continued as its president till his death in 1909.

Within the shade of three huge cherry trees of the planting brought across the plains, beside the Willamette River, I was born March 31, 1871, my mother's eighth child. An Episcopal School for girls, St. Helen's Hall, had been established by Bishop B. Wistar Morris in Portland in 1869. My sisters and I attended there and I have great-nieces of the name of Lambert attending there at the present writing, 1931.

Elizabeth's life was not all cherry blossoms and wedding cake, however. Within a few years of their marriage, Dr. Wood contracted tuberculosis, and in 1901, seeking a drier climate to help in his recuperation, they moved out of the Northwest, eventually settling in Oracle, Arizona. Although they would move back to Portland within a few years when Dr. Wood recovered his health, they continued to return to Oracle for a part of each winter.

UNTIMELY DEATHS

Their two children were Lambert Alexander, born in 1895, and Helen Henrietta, born in 1897. Both would die untimely deaths under tragic circumstances. Lambert was killed in action in July 1918 in France during the First World War. His death marked the beginning of a confused and calamitous period in Mrs. Wood's life.

In 1923, after several years of declining health, Elizabeth's beloved husband, Dr. Wood, died. About that time, Helen's marriage ended in divorce, and she moved back to Tioga with her young son. The following year, Mrs. Wood adopted Helen's son, then four years old, to raise as her own, even renaming him Lambert after her own son. Less than a year later, while on a restorative vacation voyage, Helen was lost overboard in the Indian Ocean.

In the years that followed, Elizabeth spent increasing amounts of time in Long Beach devoting herself to her grandson and pursuing her two great interests—writing and teaching Sunday school. In 1938, Lambert graduated from Ilwaco High School. He went on to the University of Arizona and, after graduation, at the onset of World War II, joined the army air forces. Then, in a cruel twist of fate, he was killed when his fighter plane crashed in Texas—the second of Mrs. Wood's Lamberts to be lost during a world war.

It may have been during that period of time that Mrs. Wood wrote this:

Possessions
Alone in the house my children loved,
I see its fireplace, with shelves above,
Its jar of shell, seaweed, smoke wood,
As things of value, since understood
To be their treasures covering years
They gathered and hoarded.
I see through tears.

Recognized since her youth for her articles and poetry, which appeared in regional publications, Mrs. Wood soon became nationally known as a successful author of juvenile books about pioneer times in the West and Northwest. Her typewriter still sits on the desk in the north dormer window of her third-floor writing studio at the Long Beach house.

THE TRAGEDY
of the
POWERS MINE

ELIZABETH LAMBERT WOOD

Wood's best-known novel, *The Tragedy of the Powers Mine*, was based on real-life events near Oracle, Arizona. *Courtesy of Candy Glenn.*

"It is in that room that I feel Mrs. Wood's presence the most," says Candy Glenn, "but it's not just upstairs that I am aware of her. The minute you enter the house you feel a wonderful, warm embrace of welcome. There is no doubt in my mind that Mrs. Wood's spirit is here and that she is thankful that we are caring for her beloved house."

Candy and her husband, Frank Glenn III, purchased the house in 1972. Their daughter, Erin Glenn, was three years old, and Sonny (Frank IV) was born shortly after the family moved in. All of the Glenns express special delight in the house and are very sentimental about it, but not all of them have the same perceptions concerning the spirit of the house.

Frank, for instance, says flat out that he has no feeling that there is a presence or a ghost in the house. "I've never felt anything like that," he says, "but it is a wonderful old house, and I like it very much."

PRESENCE OF MRS. WOOD

The other three Glenn family members have had varying sorts of interactions with Mrs. Wood over the years. Candy says that one summer day, as she walked through the front door, she heard typing upstairs. "It was very clear. I knew no one was up there, but I went up anyway. Mrs. Wood's typewriter was there on the desk—silent."

Each summer, from the time she was nine, Candy would come from Portland to the Long Beach Peninsula to stay with her grandparents, Nelse and Lottie Holmberg, whom she describes as "my salvation from a very difficult childhood."

"They owned the Dream-by-the-Sea Motel, and even though I actually worked for them each summer, the time I spent on the Peninsula was the most treasured part of my childhood. The motel was two blocks east of the Elizabeth Lambert Wood House," she remembers. "I would walk right by the house every time I went out to the ocean beach. I loved looking at the house and wondering what it was like inside and how it was furnished. I never dreamed that one day I would own it."

Frank, who grew up on the Peninsula, also remembers the house from his youth and remembers that Mrs. Wood was a sort of icon in the community. "She did a lot for Long Beach. She gave many, many books from her personal collection of children's books to the Long Beach School library. She also donated considerable acreage to the Lone Fir Cemetery and gave the land and the construction costs for the original Presbyterian church in Long Beach—the building that is just south of the Long Beach School. For years, also, she conducted very well-attended Bible study classes in her living room, and in later life, she donated that wonderful stained-glass window to the Episcopal church."

Candy says, "After Frank and I married, we were living on the bay, and we saw an ad in the paper saying that the house was for sale. I could scarcely believe it! At that point, the house was owned by Seattle residents who had purchased it after Mrs. Wood's death. We are only the third owners since the house was built 110 years ago!"

When Mrs. Wood died, she no longer had any direct heirs, so there was a search for her relatives. Over the years, she had amassed quite a fortune due

Mrs. Wood and her children, baby Helen and toddler Lambert, shown here in a studio portrait taken around 1898. *Courtesy of Candy Glenn.*

to the discovery of rich mineral deposits on her Oracle holdings. The Long Beach house was the least valuable of her properties, and her heirs, when located, worked for a speedy cash settlement. The house was put up for sale.

Two couples from Seattle bought the house at that time—just as soon as it was listed. The men had been fraternity brothers in college and were frequent visitors to the Peninsula, and all of them knew the house and loved it. They bought it in February 1964. One of the owners, Jean Maulbetsch, wrote an account of their purchase:

> To our delight, the house was completely furnished. The house was as Elizabeth Lambert Wood had lived in it and loved it. For example: personal photographs; an organ and a piano; décor items (horn birds from Africa, etc.); hundreds of books; diaries and journals; dishes, pots, tableware, etc.; rugs, antique furniture and lamps; pictures, including a huge steel engraving [were left in the house].
>
> We learned that the fireplace bricks are hunks of sailing ship ballast. Ships returning from the Orient in the mid and late 1800s were often lightly loaded with fabrics and other low-weight items. Heavy ballast was required for balance. This added weight was jettisoned at the mouth of the Columbia to reduce draft for the up-river journey to Portland.
>
> By 1973 all of our lives had so changed that having a vacation home so far from Seattle was no longer practical…We placed the house on the market and, to our delight, a lovely couple, Frank and Candy Glenn, became the owners.

"For me, there has always been an air of magic about the house," says Erin Glenn, daughter of Candy and Frank. "My earliest memories are of my playroom on the third floor—the room that had once been Mrs. Wood's writing studio. I was always fascinated by the books that are still in that room and by the photographs of Mrs. Wood and her children that are found throughout the house."

A TRAY OF GIFTS

Erin moved back into the house as an adult and vividly recalls the experience she had on one of the first two or three nights she was there. "I was asleep and a large, older woman approached and leaned over my bed. She was carrying a tray of offerings—different sorts of objects and figurines. It wasn't like a dream. I felt it was real—like it was actually happening. I knew, absolutely, that the woman was Mrs. Wood and that she was greeting me and receiving me back into the house. She was presenting me with gifts of welcome."

Erin's brother, Sonny, has not always had such positive experiences in this house of his childhood. Of the four family members, it is Sonny who has actually had some terrifying interactions with another presence—or perhaps multiple presences—of the house.

"But," he insists, "I love the house, and I loved living there, both as a child and as an adult. There's just one room I actually feel afraid of. I call it the cranberry room. It's the southeast bedroom and was always a guest room. I had a really bad experience there when I was about seven years old. I was home alone one afternoon, playing and listening to records in the cranberry room, and suddenly I felt that I was not alone. I didn't actually see anyone—at least no earthly person was there. It just began to feel heavy and stifling in there—not at all a good feeling, and I felt like running out. After that, I pretty much stayed out of that room. I was scared of it and I gave it a wide berth, even from the hallway. I felt as if someone or something might unexpectedly come out of it. I certainly never slept in it, and I don't think I ever will. I still don't have a good feeling about the room."

Sonny also spent some years in the house as an adult. Before he and his wife, Karla, moved in—and with Sonny's past experience in mind—they "smudged" the house in preparation.

"Smudging is an ancient tradition among the Native Americans and native peoples everywhere. It's a spiritual welcoming or cleansing—a refreshing. We burned a special sage plant I had gathered in Montana and walked throughout the house with it smoldering and smoking. It smelled great, and the next day the entire house felt wonderfully fresh and clean. Except for that one room. There, the smoke didn't seem to 'take.'

"I think that was the daughter Helen's room," continues Sonny. "There is some mystery about her death. Like did she fall overboard? Or did she jump? She apparently had become very depressed after her son was born and never fully recovered. That last vacation cruise with her mother was supposed to help her return to health. No matter what the story is, that particular room just isn't cheerful. There is a troubled presence there. It's not like the rest of the house."

Candy, too, concedes that the cranberry room may be a little different in feeling, but she has never had an unpleasant experience there or, for that matter, in any of the other rooms, though her son has.

SCARY EPISODES

"Actually," he says, "both Karla and I have had a few scary episodes there. In fact, during the time I was doing graduate work and was gone for long periods, Karla wouldn't stay alone in the house. She had friends stay with her or she went to her mother's.

"Ours was the master bedroom on the second floor. We spent a few 'hair-raising' nights there. At that time, I was a graduate student in the field of mental health, and among all the other ways I was growing and learning, I thought it would be a good thing to step into my own fear—confront my demons, if you will. I decided to try to be scientific about it—to open my eyes, to meditate and to see what would come.

"What happened was incredible. As I lay in bed, in the dark, eyes wide open, the air began to become dense; I could actually feel it thickening. And as I watched, it was taking a recognizable form. In through the door wafted a misty form, which began to look like an aged, wizened female. Her head was discernible and was floating toward me. She was so very old—like 150 years old. I finally had to pull the covers over my head.

"This happened three or four times, and it seemed like it started something. Both Karla and I had the experience of waking up in full consciousness but feeling paralyzed, trapped inside our bodies, not being able to move or to call out. That's a horrible feeling. It happened to each of us, not at the same time, but more than once. Then one night, I had what I can only describe as a vivid dream. A white mist floated across the threshold, and as it approached me, I gasped, which caused me to inhale it. Instantly, I was transported to the bed in the next room—the cranberry room! I had, in the dream, become Helen and the room looked like it was 1918, complete with period furniture. The feeling was so terribly unhappy. I looked toward the sea and one hundred dreary days rushed by in fast forward. I felt very depressed. Then the father of Helen's child entered the room. She was not happy with him and told him, 'I don't want you here.' After that experience, neither Karla nor I ever had the paralysis problem again."

Sonny feels sure that the maleficent presence is Helen, but he is not certain what her unhappiness is all about. "Overall, I have a good feeling in the house. Many of the rooms feel like restorative, restful places you would expect to find in a seaside home. Mrs. Wood's presence is positive and pervasive but does not wipe away the feeling of Helen's discontent, which seems centered in that cranberry room."

Right: Helen Wood died under somewhat mysterious circumstances while vacationing abroad. *Courtesy of Candy Glenn.*

Below: Elizabeth Lambert Wood on the widow's walk just above her third-story writing studio at her Long Beach home. *Courtesy of Candy Glenn.*

WORDS TO LIVE BY

On the occasion of Elizabeth Lambert Wood's eighty-fifth birthday in 1956, the *Arizona Daily Star* published an interview with her. Included were her thoughts on longevity:

Basically, have a good time at whatever you are doing or have to do...As a child I laughed often, as the eighth of 10 children. My laughing often irked others and I was frequently admonished, "When you grow older, life won't seem so funny." Glancing back over years of health and activity, I wonder if my laughing did not contribute to my sound body...

Have faith in God. I try to remember to accept His bounty with humility...

Get as much excitement out of finding the first wild strawberry in spring as in climbing a mountain or setting off for Europe...Daily whet your taste for beauty...

Pay bills promptly; keep your credit and conscience clean. Blot out disappointment in people and events...First thing in the morning, throw out the window all distaste for a job, your fellow workmen, and the world about you...

Early acknowledge that no competition confronts anyone except to outstrip himself

"Mrs. Wood had an abiding faith and was obviously a strong woman," says Candy. "She had to be to withstand all the adversity in her life and to persevere, making the well-being of children her focal point."

In addition to her benevolence in the Long Beach area, Mrs. Wood gave generously to the children and youth of Arizona. Her February 14, 1962 obituary in the *Arizona Citizen* said:

Mrs. Elizabeth Lambert Wood, 91, who donated to the Tucson YMCA a 600-acre ranch near Oracle which became the Triangle Y Ranch Camp, died this morning at the San Manuel Hospital. She had suffered a stroke Friday night.

Illness prevented her from attending the annual YMCA dinner Monday night at which she was to be honored for her life-long services to youth.

Mrs. Wood maintained a home for her use on the Y Camp ranch where she has lived with a woman companion [Hulda Foresman] for the past 25 years. She also maintained a home at Long Beach, Wash. where she had spent much of her earlier life. Her husband was a well-known physician in that area.

A pioneer rancher of the Oracle mountain area, in 1949 she gave the Crooked G. (now the YMCA camp), as a memorial to her son and grandson. At the time it was recognized as a $40,000 gift.

It was not her only gift to Tucson. In 1938, she gave Pepper Sauce Canyon, in the same area, to the city as a camp ground and a recreation area for children. Later, it became a Salvation Army district camp.

Known as a philanthropist wherever she lived, it is said that tragedy led Mrs. Wood into doing more than the average person to better the lot of children.

"I'm sure she spent many hours up on the widow's walk," says Candy, "though not for the traditional reason of watching for the return of a ship. I think the vista out to sea must have been a solace to her. And I know she loved this house, as we do. She wrote this poem. It's my favorite. I know it's about this house."

There's a house
Whose rooms
I know by heart.

Where I tended the garden
And read my books.

Where dreams were dreamt
And memories made.

Where children grew up
And I grew old

There's a house
Where life was lived

A house
Where I belong.

11

THE LIGHT KEEPER'S WIFE

Mary Pesonen had put in twenty-five long years as the keeper's wife at the North Head lighthouse. For all that time, she had endured isolation and loneliness. She had persevered through the gales of winter and through endless days of murky fog and relentless rain. She had cooked and cleaned, cared for the animals and tended the gardens. And just the previous week, she had received a clean bill of health from her Portland doctor.

So why, on the morning of June 9, 1923, did she choose to end her life? According to her obituary in the *Ilwaco Tribune* a few days later, her death "occurred last Saturday morning when she threw herself over the towering cliffs at North Head and dashed herself to death on the jagged rocks below."

The mystery was further complicated by her husband's report that she had seemed exceptionally cheerful the evening beforehand. They had returned just that day, after Mary had undergone some weeks of medical treatment for a "mental breakdown," thought to be the culmination of many months of depression, or "melancholia," as it was termed in those years.

On Saturday morning—her last, as it turned out—she got up at five o'clock, telling her husband to stay in bed for a bit. She was going to do some errands and take a walk, as was her custom and an activity advised by her doctor. A short while later, the dog, always a companion on her walks, returned, but Mary did not. It was the "queer antics" of the dog that alerted Alex Pesonen to the possibility of trouble.

Said her obituary:

North Head lighthouse near Cape Disappointment, Washington, sits 130 feet above the Pacific Ocean. *Courtesy of Washington State Parks.*

He notified the boys at the radio station and also at the weather bureau, and a searching party was soon organized. The dog led searchers to a spot just under the fire control station near the North Head lighthouse, and there they found her coat lying on the edge of the cliff. A trail through the tall grass, as though someone had slid down the cliff, was mute evidence of what had befallen the unfortunate woman.

More help was sent for, this time from Ilwaco and Fort Canby. "Blasting was resorted to but nothing came of it," continued the obituary, "until about five o'clock in the evening, when Frank Hammond, one of the assistant keepers at North Head light, found the body lying in a little cove just beyond the Pesonen garden, where it had drifted with the tide."

RETIREMENT IN SIX MONTHS

Compounding the mystery of why Mary chose that particular Saturday to end her life is the fact that Alex was due to retire in just six months. Their intention was to develop a piece of cranberry land that they owned near Shoalwater Bay and to spend their winters in California—certainly aspirations to look forward to after all those years in the lighthouse service.

Facts about Mary Pesonen are meager. They come mainly from the *Tribune* obituary, although at least one of those is questionable. She was said to be fifty-four years of age, but her tombstone in the Ilwaco cemetery shows her birth in 1870 and her death in 1923, making her, at the most, fifty-three years old—eleven years younger than her husband. Her maiden name was Watson, and she was a native of Ireland. She and Alexander K. Pesonen had been married for twenty-seven years. As far as is known, the couple had no children.

The tombstone of Alexander and Mary Watson Pesonen is in the Ilwaco Cemetery, not far from the North Head lighthouse. *Photo by Jon Christian.*

Alexander K. Pesonen was the first light keeper at North Head and began his tenure there on the long-awaited day the light was put into service. It had been forty-two years since the Cape Disappointment light, just two miles distant, had gone into service. On that day in 1856, it was the hope that the beams sent out from the "Cape D" light would be sufficient to quell the shipwrecks in the treacherous waters around the Columbia River bar. They were so common that the area had long been called "The Graveyard of the Pacific."*

Unfortunately though, it was soon apparent that the Cape Disappointment lighthouse beacon was obscured to ships approaching from the north by McKenzie Head, which extends southwest from Cape Disappointment. Little attention was given to the problem, however. It was only due to the evidence of the many wrecks along the Long Beach Peninsula, in combination with a plea from the United States Lighthouse Board, that money for the project was finally appropriated. German-born engineer C.W. Leick was hired to design the tower and other necessary buildings.

Construction was begun in 1897, and though it was beset by delays, the lighthouse was completed and the lamp lit on May 16, 1898. George Langford, an early contractor and builder from Portland, Oregon, was in charge of the project. Capped with a red roof, the white 65-foot conical tower was built on a 130-foot cliff of solid basalt and faced directly out to the Pacific. The building itself was simple. Downstairs was a single room, which served as a workroom and storage area, and up the sixty-nine steps was the lens room and gallery.

The original lens was a first-order (non-flashing) Fresnel (pronounced Fray-nel), manufactured in France in 1822. The lens had originally been used at the Navesink lighthouse in New Jersey and later in San Francisco and at Cape Disappointment. Its light source was a five-wick oil lamp, eighteen inches across the base and over eight feet high. It had a beam of 3.5 million candlepower, bright enough to be seen twenty miles at sea—bright enough, the light service hoped, to provide ample warning to ships coming from the north.†

---

* According to James A. Gibbs in his definitive 1950 book, *Pacific Graveyard*: "The number of vessels which have sustained damage or been lost in this graveyard of the Pacific—including deep-sea vessels, harbor craft, and fishing boats—would likely exceed two thousand, with more than fifteen hundred lives claimed."
† In 1935, the first-order lens was replaced by a fourth-order lens. That lens was eventually replaced by an aerobeacon in the 1950s and later by a modern optic, mounted outside the tower. The light was automated in 1961.

The earliest known photograph of North Head lighthouse and the oil houses shows them under construction (circa 1898). *Courtesy of Washington State Parks.*

Concurrent with the construction of the lighthouse, workers built two oil houses just to the east. A keeper's residence, a duplex to house two assistant keepers, a barn and outbuildings were also constructed at that time.* No sooner was the work completed than Alex and Mary moved in.

A Keeper's Duties

The Light Keeper's main duty was to make sure that the light operated each night between sunset and sunrise. By day, he scoured and polished the glass prisms of the light, and by night, he tended the burning oil. It required a degree of physical strength and consistent attention, but in the main, it was a repetitive, monotonous job. George Easterbrook, light keeper at the nearby Cape D, wrote this description of his 1893 job:

* All of the original buildings are still located on site. In 2013, the United States Coast Guard officially transferred ownership of the lighthouse and the buildings to Washington State Parks. The keeper's and assistant keepers' houses are available for vacation rentals.

To wind up the weights of the clockwork machinery that kept the pumps in motion, pumping up oil from the reservoir to the summit of the wicks in the burners, then falling back whence it came, and continuing this flow the whole night through, ours being a first order stationary light, with five concentric wicks, giving a solid mass of light almost rivaling the sun, and surrounded by an open lantern of heavy French glass prisms, and all inclosed [sic] by windows of heavy plate glass, with a space or inside gallery between them and the lantern itself. I at once sprang up the short flight of iron steps and into the lantern, and fixing on the crank to the oil clock, wound it up snug and gave it another two hours' safe run.

I then went at my next regular duty, which was to carefully wipe each prism in the lantern and their reflectors, with fine chamois skin, and to clean the inside of the plate windows with towels for that purpose, which labor takes generally two hours, and then comes a rest for the balance of the watch, except on such nights as these, when the salt spray of the ocean, being caught up by the storm and dashed against the glass outside, soon coats it over with a film of salt and grime, which must be cleared off as soon as possible or the light is so obscured as to be of little service.

This residence, now a vacation rental, was occupied by North Head light keepers and their families from 1898 to 1961. *Photo by Jon Christian.*

Until 1910, the lighthouses and light keepers at Cape Disappointment and North Head, like those throughout the United States, fell under the jurisdiction of a federal agency called the lighthouse board. After that time, the United States Lighthouse Service, also known as the Bureau of Lighthouses, was responsible for the upkeep and maintenance of the facilities. In 1939, the responsibility for the lighthouses was transferred to the United States Coast Guard, under whose jurisdiction many lighthouses remain today.

The duties of the light keepers were clearly laid out, and they were evaluated periodically by vigorous inspections. The average salary of a light keeper in 1900 was about $800 per year. Wives of lighthouse keepers were also subject to inspections, and though they were not paid for their domestic duties, their strengths or weaknesses were reflected in the ratings of their husbands.

Donna Gabriel Oman (1921–2008) of Long Beach grew up at the North Head lighthouse. Her father was light keeper there directly following Alex Pesonen's retirement. Donna's mother, like Mary Pesonen, was Irish, and in an interview in 2006, Donna remembered that "she had a lot of energy. When she got frustrated or upset about things, she would take it out on the floor. She'd get down on her hands and knees and scrub it with a scrubbing brush until it gleamed.

"I think she was a good homemaker and housekeeper, but once, when I was about to leave for school, the government inspector arrived at the door. He hadn't given any warning, and my mother had just stripped all the beds, getting ready to do the wash. She kicked things out of the way for the inspection, but he noticed everything, and my dad got marked down on the report. They were very strict."

In those years before electricity and running water, the work involved in maintaining a household in the storm-lashed isolation of North Head was considerable. The domestic duties of the light keeper's wife included far more than the usual cooking, cleaning, sewing and other household chores. Her responsibilities also included caring for the garden and animals (probably chickens, a cow and several horses at the very least), cleaning the privy and keeping the outbuildings and grounds neatly maintained. It was also her duty to oversee the domestic affairs for the assistant keepers who lived in the

This aerial photograph of the buildings at North Head shows, in the distance at right, the lighthouse overlooking the Pacific Ocean. *Courtesy of Washington State Parks.*

duplex next door.* For a woman subject to melancholia, the responsibilities may have seemed overwhelming.

No doubt Alex's standards for his wife were high as well. He came to North Head with a reputation as something of a hero. Born in Finland in 1859, he immigrated to America in 1876 and made his way to the Columbia. He first served on the tender *Manzanita* and then as a keeper of the famous "Terrible Tillie"—Tillamook Rock Lighthouse at Tillamook, Oregon. During his eight years there, he saved the lighthouse from a severe storm that threatened to sweep it out to sea. While at North Head, he was awarded the lighthouse-efficiency flag for having the model station in the district.

---

* According to one light keeper's story about the three residences—those of the light keeper and of the first and second assistants—they were identical except for the chandeliers. The head keeper's residence had a six-candle chandelier, while those in the first and second assistants' homes each had only five and four candles respectively.

DISTURBANCES AT THE KEEPER'S HOUSE

Except for the report concerning her hospital stay in Portland, however, there is no indication of Mary's general emotional state during the twenty-five years she was at the lighthouse. After her death, it would be another seven decades before the first disturbances at the light keeper's house were reported. That was long after the house had been lived in by light keepers and their families.

It was in 1961, when the light at North Head became fully automatic, that the two light-keeper houses were converted to state park offices and park ranger housing. In 2000, the charming historic homes became vacation rentals. Each has three bedrooms, one bath, period furniture and a full kitchen with many modern-day conveniences. As their popularity has increased, so have the reports of strange activities in the keeper's house and on the grounds.

Although reports of a presence are vague, interest runs high and queries are persistent—"I get at least one question a day," said one of the volunteer

Are Mary and Alex Pesonen among those who watch as the grounded *Columbia River Lightship No. 50* is hauled across Cape Disappointment Isthmus to Baker Bay in March 1901? *Courtesy of Washington State Parks.*

lighthouse interpreters in a recent interview by local newspaper insert the *Coast Weekend*. There have been murmurs about a shadowy figure on the grounds and reports of blinking lights and other mysterious electrical phenomena at the keeper's house. Perhaps it is the persistence of those reports that has prompted park personnel to be on the lookout for pictures of Mary and Alex.

The only possibility that has surfaced so far is a photograph taken in March 1901, just short of three years after Alex and Mary took up residence at North Head. The picture shows the *Columbia River Lightship No. 50*, which had been ripped from its moorings in a storm and grounded on the beach at McKenzie Head far below the North Head light.

The ship is being hauled across the Cape Disappointment Isthmus to Baker Bay. A crowd has gathered to watch the activity, and speculation is that Alex and Mary Pesonen are the man and woman just to the left of center, he wearing a rather rumpled suit and she in a bonnet with her head turned away from the camera. Their identities are only a guess, but the shape of his hat and its insignia appear to be United States Lighthouse Service issue. For reasons not quite logical, the two seem to be a couple.

Visitors to the lighthouse continue to wonder what really happened that long-ago Saturday morning. After all this time, is Mary finally trying to tell her story? But just like the fog that shrouds the basalt cliffs of North Head most days of the year, mystery clings to Mary Pesonen, the light keeper's wife. So far, her story is incomplete.

BIBLIOGRAPHY

NEWSPAPERS

Arizona Citizen
Arizona Daily Star
Chinook Observer
Coast Weekend, Arts and Entertainment
Ilwaco Tribune
South Bend Journal

BOOKS

Baker, J.C. *Baptist History of the North Pacific Coast*. Philadelphia: Baptist Publication Society, 1912.

Davis, Charlotte. *They Remembered*. Vol. 4. Long Beach, WA: Midway Printery, 1994.

Davis, Charlotte, and Edgar Davis. *They Remembered*. 3 vols. Ilwaco, WA: Pacific Printing, 1981–1992.

Feagans, Raymond. *The Railroad that Ran by the Tide*. Berkeley, CA: Howell North Books, 1972.

Gibbs, James A. *Pacific Graveyard*. Portland, OR: Binfords & Mort, 1973.

Hazeltine, Jean. *Willapa Bay, Its Historical and Regional Geography*. South Bend, WA: South Bend Journal, 1956.

Lloyd, Nancy. *Observing Our Peninsula's Past*. 2 vols. Long Beach, WA: Chinook Observer, 2003–2006.

McDonald, Lucile. *Coast Country: A History of Southwest Washington*. Portland, OR: Binfords & Mort, 1966.

Oesting, Marie. *Oysterville Cemetery Sketches.* Ocean Park, WA: 1988.

Owens-Adair, Bethenia Angelina. *Dr. Owens-Adair: Some of Her Life Experiences.* Portland, OR: Mann & Beach, 1906.

Sherwood, Millie. *To Know What Dream.* Philadelphia: Dorrance & Company, Inc., 1955.

Williams, John G. *Johnny Stories, Scenes from My Boyhood in Old Ilwaco.* Ilwaco, WA: Pacific Printing Company, 1987.

MAGAZINES

The Sou'wester, Quarterly Magazine of the Pacific County Historical Society 9, no. 2 (1974); 10, no. 4 (1975); 12 (1977); 16, no. 4 (1981); 26, nos. 2–3 (1991); 22, no. 2 (1997); 36, no. 3 (2001); 60, no. 4 (2005); 61, no. 1 (2006).

OFFICIAL RECORDS

Department of the Interior. U.S. Board on Geographic Names, 1950.

Office of Archaeology and Historic Preservation. National Register of Historic Places. Washington, D.C., 1976.

Oysterville Baptist Church Records 1892–1980, Espy Family Archives, Oysterville and Tacoma.

Oysterville Cemetery Association. "Old Linen Map." 1905.

Statutes of the Territory of Washington, 1854. Olympia, WA, 1855.

United States Federal Census. Pacific County, Washington, 1860.

ARCHIVES AND WEBSITES

Claflin, Jim. "Collecting Nautical Antiques." *Lighthouse Digest Magazine,* December 2004, Foghorn Publishing. www.lighthousedigest.com.

Espy Family Archives. Washington State Historical Society Research Center, Tacoma, WA.

Legends of America. "Washington State Legends: Whitman Massacre National Historic." Edited by Kathy Weiser. www.legendsofamerica.com/wa-whitmanmassacre.html.

Medora Espy Archive. Washington State Historical Society Research Center, Tacoma, WA.

National Park Service Website. Whitman Mission National Historic Site. http://www.nps.gov/whmi/index.htm.

Wood, Elizabeth Lambert. "A Sketch of the Life of Elizabeth Lambert Wood." Tucson: Arizona Historical Society Library and Archives, 1931.

INDEX

ABOUT THE AUTHOR

Photo by Nyel Stevens.

It's undoubtedly genetic," laughs author and historian Sydney Stevens concerning her interest in the history of Pacific County, Washington. "Since 1854, when my great-grandfather, Robert Hamilton Espy, co-founded the town of Oysterville, there have been Espys here involved in the community and making their contributions to Long Beach Peninsula history." Sydney lives with her husband, Nyel, across from the historic Oysterville Church in the house where her parents and grandparents lived before her. In addition to her participation in local activities, she devotes much of her time to researching and documenting the history and folklore of the area. "It's a family legacy. I grew up listening to the old-timers tell about the early days here, and as the years have passed, I find myself repeating the same wonderful tales. Especially the ghost stories!"

Visit us at
www.historypress.net
....
This title is also available as an e-book